BFI FILM CLASSICS

· ·

Edward Buscombe
SERIES EDITOR

Colin MacCabe and David Meeker
SERIES CONSULTANTS

Cinema is a fragile medium. Many of the great classic films of the past now exist, if at all, in damaged or incomplete prints. Concerned about the deterioration in the physical state of our film heritage, the National Film and Television Archive, a Division of the British Film Institute, has compiled a list of 360 key films in the history of the cinema. The long-term goal of the Archive is to build a collection of perfect show-prints of these films, which will then be screened regularly at the Museum of the Moving Image in London in a year-round repertory.

BFI Film Classics is a series of books commissioned to stand alongside these titles. Authors, including film critics and scholars, film-makers, novelists, historians and those distinguished in the arts, have been invited to write on a film of their choice, drawn from the Archive's list. Each volume presents the author's own insights into the chosen film, together with a brief production history and a detailed filmography, notes and bibliography. The numerous illustrations have been specially made from the Archive's own prints.

With new titles published each year, the BFI Film Classics series will rapidly grow into an authoritative and highly readable guide to the great films of world cinema.

Could scarcely be improved upon ... informative, intelligent, jargon-free companions.
The Observer

Cannily but elegantly packaged BFI Classics will make for a neat addition to the most discerning shelves.
New Statesman & Society

D1146930

Ingmar Bergman and his daughter Lena during the shooting of *Wild Strawberries*

BFI FILM

CLASSICS

WILD STRAWBERRIES
(SMULTRONSTÄLLET)

....

Philip & Kersti French

BRITISH FILM INSTITUTE

bfi

BFI PUBLISHING

First published in 1995 by the
BRITISH FILM INSTITUTE
21 Stephen Street, London WIP 2LN

Copyright © Philip and Kersti French 1995

The British Film Institute exists
to promote appreciation, enjoyment, protection and
development of moving image culture in and throughout
the whole of the United Kingdom.
Its activities include the National Film and
Television Archive; the National Film Theatre;
the Museum of the Moving Image;
the London Film Festival; the production and
distribution of film and video; funding and
support for regional activities;
Stills, Posters and Designs; Research;
Publishing and Education; and the monthly
Sight and Sound magazine.

British Library Cataloguing-in-Publication Data
A catalogue record for this book is available from the British Library

ISBN 0-85170-481-6

Designed by
Andrew Barron & Collis Clements Associates

Typesetting by
Fakenham Photosetting Limited, Norfolk

Printed in Great Britain by
The Trinity Press, Worcester

CONTENTS

My view is, I'm the sum of everything I've read, seen, heard and experienced. I don't believe that an artist has his roots in the air. I regard myself as a little brick in a big building, dependent on what is on either side of me, under me, and behind me.

Ingmar Bergman, *Bergman on Bergman*

ACKNOWLEDGMENTS
....

We would like to thank Anders Clason, Counsellor for Cultural Affairs, and his staff at the Swedish Embassy in London, the Swedish Film Institute in Stockholm and Karlstad Public Library in Värmland for their valuable help during the writing of this book. Bertil Gejrot, Sean French and Karl French read our text and made useful suggestions. For the illustrations we are grateful to the Stills, Posters and Designs Department of the British Film Institute, Elisabet Helge of the Swedish Film Institute, the Rasmus Meyers Samlinger, Bergen, the Munch-museet, Oslo, and the Nationalmuseum, Stockholm.

The original poster for *Wild Strawberries*

1
....
SJÖSTRÖM AND BERGMAN

Wild Strawberries brings together the dominant figure of the Swedish cinema's Golden Age and the pre-eminent figure of its second flowering. They could almost be considered the film's joint auteurs.

The Golden Age of the Swedish cinema began in 1913, lasted a decade, and was overwhelmingly the creation of two charismatic, strikingly handsome directors, Victor Sjöström (1879–1960) and Mauritz Stiller (1883–1928). They were, as actors and producers, men of the theatre and neither had much in the way of formal education. Both worked for the company that produced, distributed and exhibited their films. It had been founded in 1905 and became known as Svensk Bio in 1909. In 1919 it merged with its chief rival AB Skandia, and took the name by which it is still known, Svensk Filmindustri (SF). Sjöström and Stiller frequently worked with the same cameraman, the masterly Julius Jaenzon (1885–1961), who styled himself J. Julius, and sometimes with his brother, Henrik. Five of Sjöström's finest films and three of Stiller's were based on novels by Selma Lagerlöf, who in 1909 became the first woman (and the first Swede) to win the Nobel Prize for literature. Like Sjöström, she was a native of and devoted to the largely rural province of Värmland.

Sjöström acted in most of his own movies as well as several of Stiller's. With his large head and square thrusting jaw he was a forceful presence, and he soon became a popular star. His films dealt with social injustice, prejudice, redemption, revenge and eternal love, frequently in rural and historical settings making extensive use of natural locations, and more often than not the tone and conclusion were tragic. By the early 1920s his renown was matched only by Griffith and Chaplin, who called him 'the greatest director in the world'.[1] Thus the Swedish cinema as a presence on the world scene (though not as a local industry) came to an abrupt end when Sjöström went to Hollywood in 1923, and Stiller followed him there the following year, accompanied by Greta Garbo, the star of his masterpiece, *Gösta Berlings Saga* (*The Atonement of Gösta Berling*).

Sjöström's name was changed by his Hollywood employers to Seastrom and, working in a country where he had spent several years as a child and mastered the language, he thrived, making such silent classics as *He Who Gets Slapped* (1924), *The Scarlet Letter* (1926) and *The Wind* (1928), the second and third of these starring Griffith's discovery, Lillian Gish. *The Wind*, however, possibly his greatest film, proved a box-office disaster. He directed Garbo in *The Divine Woman* (1929), of which no print is known to exist, and made one sound movie, *A Lady in Love* (1929), before returning to Sweden for good at the age of fifty. Stiller, on the other hand, did not prosper in Hollywood, putting his name to a mere three films, one of which, *The Street of Sin* (1928), was completed by Josef von Sternberg. He died at the age of forty-five, shortly after directing the musical *Broadway* on the Stockholm stage.

Sjöström directed only two further films – *The Markurells of Wadköping* (1930) in Sweden and *Under the Red Robe* (1936) in Britain – neither of them a critical or commercial success. He continued to work in the cinema as an actor and resumed the successful theatrical career that had been set aside when he went to America.

In 1942, at the age of sixty-three, Sjöström was recalled to his old company when the scholarly Carl Anders Dymling (1898–1961), as head of Sveriges Radio the equivalent figure to the BBC's Sir John Reith, was appointed Managing Director of Svensk Filmindustri. Dymling brought in Sjöström as SF's Artistic Manager and both men were to play a role in the cinematic career of Ingmar Bergman.

Born in the university town of Uppsala in 1918, Bergman grew up in Stockholm where his father, Erik Bergman, a Lutheran pastor of ferociously intimidating mien, was appointed vicar of the fashionable Hedvig Eleonora church and later, apparently through the personal intervention of the Swedish Queen Viktoria, who had heard him preach there, made chaplain of the Royal Hospital, Sofiahemmet. After graduating from Stockholm University, Bergman continued to pursue his passionate interest in the theatre and attempted to establish himself as a writer. An amateur production of a play of his was seen by Stina Bergman, head of the script department at SF, and she engaged him as a reader and adapter. The widow of the distinguished playwright and novelist Hjalmar Bergman (no relation to Ingmar), she and her husband were among Sjöström's closest friends and had accompanied him to Hollywood in 1923. This was not, however, a happy time for young Ingmar Bergman. He was making little progress as an author, had cut himself off from his overbearing parents and, despite being nearly penniless, had embarked on the first of his five marriages. Sixteen years later this first wife, Else Fisher, would be the choreographer on *The Seventh Seal* and would play the hero's mother as a young woman in the final flashback of *Wild Strawberries*.

For a couple of years, Bergman's screenplay *Hets* (*Frenzy*) had been lying around the studio until there was a sudden demand for a suitable script to be directed by Alf Sjöberg as part of a programme of prestigious pictures to mark the twenty-fifth anniversary of the founding of SF. It is not without a certain piquancy that Bergman and Sjöström should have been brought together to celebrate a genuine Silver Jubilee and that their association should reach its peak in a fictional Golden Jubilee. In October 1943, Sjöström gave a press conference announcing SF's forthcoming project, a report of which in the Stockholm newspaper *Social-Demokraten* is probably the first public mention of Bergman in relation to cinema.[2]

> Ingmar Bergman has written a screenplay, which will be put into production after the comedy *His Official Fiancée*. His original story is called *Frenzy*; it deals with the pressures of exams in a school's final year and with the relationship between teacher and pupil in a Stockholm high school. Experimentally inclined, but obviously written with talent, in Sjöström's opinion.

It is a mark of Sjöström's respect for Bergman that when he was asked by the press for some words of appreciation of the Danish writer Kaj Munk following his murder by the Nazis in early 1944 (Sjöström had appeared the previous year in a film of Munk's play *Ordet*, directed by Gustaf Molander), he asked the young writer to prepare a draft for him.

Sjöström took a close interest in *Frenzy* (1944) and it became the major film of the SF jubilee and the most celebrated Swedish movie of the decade. While it was in production, the 26-year-old Bergman was appointed Artistic Director of the City Theatre of Helsingborg, a town on the south coast of Sweden, separated only by a narrow strip of water from Elsinore in Denmark. It lies between Gothenburg and Malmö (although a great deal closer to the latter), and these three places were to be the centres of his theatrical work over the next fifteen years. He was the youngest person ever to hold this post.

In the summer of 1945, after a hectic season producing ten plays at Helsingborg, Bergman returned to SF in Stockholm to direct his first movie, *Crisis*, based on a Danish play not of his own choosing. It proved an unrelievedly painful experience and the picture turned out a critical and financial disaster. That Bergman didn't abandon the project was due to the support of Dymling (who suggested he start all over again after the first three weeks) and Sjöström (who kept turning up with practical advice and encouragement). Sjöström noted in his diary: 'Touchy moments with Ingmar Bergman, who is extremely sensitive and lets himself be easily thrown off balance.'[3] As Bergman recalls it:[4]

> He grabbed me firmly by the nape of my neck and walked me like that back and forth across the asphalted area outside the studio, mostly in silence, but suddenly he was saying things that were simple and comprehensible. You make your scenes too complicated ... Work more simply. Film the actors from the front. They like that and it's best that way. Don't keep having rows with everyone. They simply get angry and do a less good job.

1 2   (l. to r.) Ingmar Bergman, Bibi Andersson, Victor Sjöström and cameraman Gunnar Fischer on location

The firm hand of Sjöström must have reminded Bergman of his father, and indeed there is a certain physical resemblance between these two stern, moustachioed men. It is also the case that Sjöström's own father, though never ordained, became a domineering religious zealot.

Bergman was subsequently exiled from SF and made his next three pictures for other companies. These first four films were in the poetic-realist manner of the prewar work of Julien Duvivier and Marcel Carné. On his return to SF he showed that he had fallen under the influence of Italian neo-realism, and his fourth film back there reunited him with Victor Sjöström. In *Till Glädje* (*To Joy*, 1949), Sjöström plays a celebrated conductor, father figure to a wilful violinist and his musician wife, members of the same symphony orchestra in Helsingborg. The picture manifestly reflects Bergman's career in the theatre, his experience of parenthood, the breakdown of his second marriage, and the tug between domestic life and artistic vocation. It is also the third of his sixteen collaborations, all of them in black-and-white, with Gunnar Fischer, an outstanding cinematographer who joined SF in 1936 as an assistant to Julius Jaenzon. In addition, as Peter Cowie has pointed out, *To Joy* is the first of Bergman's pictures to exploit the particular luminous quality of the light of the Swedish summer, and in his view contains more cinematic poetry than the sum of his previous films.[5]

Nearly ten years would pass before Bergman and Sjöström worked together again – in 1957 on *Wild Strawberries*. By that time Bergman had entered the third stylistic phase of his career, which he attributes in part to his discovery of German Expressionism during a sojourn in Paris in 1949 when he haunted both the Comédie Française and the Cinémathèque. This became a marked influence in *Gycklarnas Afton* (*Sawdust and Tinsel*, 1953), the first of his films that might be considered a masterpiece and the first to attract serious attention outside Scandinavia. Two Swedish directors, Gustaf Molander (1888–1973) and Alf Sjöberg (1903–80), created reputable bodies of work between the silent Golden Age and the 1950s, and Bergman wrote screenplays for both of them. But the second flowering of the Swedish cinema can be said to date from the early 1950s – from Sjöberg's *Fröken Julie* (*Miss Julie*), which won the Palme d'Or at Cannes in 1951, Arne Mattsson's *Hon dansade en sommar* (*One Summer of Happiness*, 1951), Arne Sucksdorff's *Det Stora Äventyret* (*The Great Adventure*, 1953), and Bergman's *Sawdust and Tinsel*.

2
....

A SWEDISH ODYSSEY

Wild Strawberries begins with Professor Eberhard Isak Borg, Professor Emeritus of Bacteriology at, presumably, the Karolinska Institute in Stockholm, speaking rather smugly about his life, as the camera pans around the elegant book-lined study of the comfortable Stockholm apartment he shares with his 74-year-old housekeeper of many years, Miss Agda, and a Great Dane that is unnamed and goes unremarked upon. As he announces himself as a misanthropic loner, apparently content with a life apart from a somewhat distasteful humanity, the camera picks up framed photographs of people we will meet later on – his 96-year-old mother, his son Evald, his daughter-in-law Marianne, his long-dead wife Karin. We also see a chess set, which in the context of Bergman's career, a year after *The Seventh Seal*, hints at another encounter with Death. Isak Borg is a 78-year-old widower; Evald, his only child, a lecturer in medicine at the University of Lund, is 38 – the same ages respectively of Victor Sjöström and Ingmar Bergman when the movie was made. Isak, we learn later, is the fourth oldest of ten brothers and sisters, all but himself now dead.

Borg's initials, EIB, are the same as Ernst Ingmar Bergman's and the name Isak Borg suggests in Swedish, and more or less translates into English, as Ice Fortress. Isaac was the son that Abraham (in Genesis 22: 1–12) was prepared to sacrifice to God, and his mother was Sarah, the name of Borg's lost love and the woman in the present who brings her to mind. In one of the most celebrated set pieces in August Strindberg's early satirical novel *The Red Room* (1879), a cynical medical student called Borg helps escort a coffin with a blank name-plate, borne by a horse-drawn hearse from a house in one of Stockholm's less salubrious southern districts, to the cemetery. (This particular Borg, an anti-semite, insists on addressing a Jewish fellow mourner called Levi as 'Isaac'.) More important, perhaps, it is the name of the overbearing, Nietzschean protagonist of Strindberg's *By the Open Sea* (*I Havsbandet*, 1890), a young scientist sent to advise primitive, unappreciative fishermen. 'God preserve us from so self-important and egocentric a man', wrote the contemporary reviewer for the right-wing Stockholm daily *Svenska Dagbladet*; but the character of Borg was much admired by Franz Kafka.[6] Bergman was to use the name a decade later in *Hour of the*

Wolf, where Max von Sydow plays Johan Borg.

Wild Strawberries is in effect an extended flashback, with flashbacks and dreams within that flashback, covering a single day, Saturday, 1 June, presumably in 1957, of special importance to Borg. (The earlier *Sawdust and Tinsel* and the later *Winter Light* have a similar time-scale.) Bergman, however, fudges this between writing the script and making the movie, and the time scheme remains vague to all but the most assiduous viewer. In the original screenplay, Borg, after introducing himself and his family, says:

> Later I will come back to the reason for writing this story, which is, as nearly as I can make it, a true account of the events, dreams and thoughts which befell me on a certain day.[7]

In the film, Bergman destroys or undermines this narrative framework by having Borg announce before the credits that 'Tomorrow at Lund I will celebrate the fiftieth anniversary of my doctorate.' Borg would have gained two earlier degrees of *medicine kandidat* and *medicine licentiat.* To obtain these he would have done eight years of medical studies and would have been qualified to practise medicine. He had continued, however, to a full doctorate *(medicine doktor),* a peculiarly exacting degree in Swedish universities and both rarer and more demanding than a doctorate in the English-speaking world. The practice was established at Sweden's two ancient universities, Uppsala, founded in 1477, and Lund, founded in 1688 (it has now been adopted by the country's newer seats of learning), that those who obtain this degree and survive for a further fifty years are invited to return for the honorary accolade of *jubeldoktor* or 'jubilee doctor', a reward for both academic distinction and longevity. The majority of such honorees are octogenarians and Isak is somewhat younger, a further reason for Bergman to have added two years to his age as given in the draft of the screenplay. Bergman has not, however, corrected the date for the ancient ceremony at Lund, which should have been the last day of May, and he has exercised his poet's licence in shifting the ceremony from its traditional time of midday to early evening.

Borg had planned to make the journey by plane, flying from Stockholm to Malmö, a little south of Lund, his alma mater – an uncommon thing to do in those days. For Miss Agda, his elderly

housekeeper, the flight would have been part of the exotic experience. But the credit titles are followed by a disturbing nightmare in which Borg sees a clock without hands outside a watchmaker's shop, examines his own handless watch, meets a faceless man resembling a foetus, and is nearly knocked over when a horse-drawn hearse without a coachman goes out of control and sheds a wheel. The coffin that crashes to the ground opens and a hand reaches out to grasp Borg's hand. The corpse is that of Borg himself. This, the first of the film's five departures from the present, or from everyday reality, persuades Borg to make the journey by road. Not of course because he has received any admonitory signals about the flight. What he has been given is a graphic intimation of imminent mortality that suggests he should revisit the scenes of his earlier life before it is too late.

The journey he decides to undertake is a fairly arduous one. On the Swedish roads of 1957 it would have been well over 600 kilometres, roughly the distance from London to Edinburgh, and demanding around a dozen hours by Borg's reckoning. The current Shell map, charting some of the best, least crowded roads in Western Europe, still recommends some 7½ hours for a drive from Stockholm to Malmö.

Victor Sjöström in *The Phantom Carriage*

This journey, almost exactly south-west from Stockholm to the southernmost part of the Kattegat opposite Copenhagen, was the sharpest angle of Bergman's professional axis between Stockholm, his home town, the centre of movie-making and the national capital, and those southern cities where he pursued his art as a driven, innovative man of the theatre. Several of his early films are set down there, or begin in Stockholm and end up in the south-west: *Hamnstad* (1948), *To Joy* (1949), *A Lesson in Love* (1953), *A Journey into Autumn* (1955). And numerous movies from his first decade as a director involve significant railway journeys (in *Waiting Women* Bergman makes a Hitchcockian appearance in the corridor of a train taking his characters to the south-west). *Wild Strawberries* is his first movie where the automobile is a significant form of transport and the only one featuring an extended car journey, though the pastor drives from church to church in *Winter Light*, an important dramatic revelation occurs at the driving wheel in *Persona*, and a traumatic motor accident lies behind *A Passion*. But after *Wild Strawberries* few characters in Bergman's films travel long distances (*The Silence* is the principal exception); in most cases they hardly travel at all.

Time is very important in *Wild Strawberries*: the booming crack of doom that introduces the film; the images of time suspended in the nightmare. Borg makes his decision to go by road at 3 a.m. (a clock in the apartment sounds the hour), and as he drives through a sleeping central Stockholm a municipal clock rings out the hour. Leaving behind Miss Agda to take the plane, Isak is accompanied by his daughter-in-law – and essential co-driver – Marianne. It transpires that Marianne is estranged from Evald and expecting a child he does not want, domestic matters she has found impossible to discuss with the distant, fastidious Borg. Central to Evald's problems, however, is the large, still unrepaid loan from his father that allowed him to complete his studies. (This phenomenon of the loan from a bank or, as here, from a parent, to see someone through lengthy academic studies was the norm rather than the exception in those days, though it puzzled audiences in the English-speaking world. Most Swedish students still borrow money, although nowadays from the state.)

The professor's car is a large, pre-war American sedan, seating seven comfortably with its jump-seats. It is a 1937 Packard Twelve 7-Passenger limo, a fashionable car of its time and now a collectors' item. (It is to be distinguished from the 1938 Packard Twelve, which had a split windscreen.) In its size and imposing solemnity, this car clearly echoes the hearse of the opening nightmare. Like Borg, it is an elegant relic of the past, a point that is specifically made later on.

Observant younger moviegoers may be surprised by the fact that Borg and Marianne drive their left-hand-drive car on the left of the road. It was only in September 1969 that Sweden fell into line with Continental Europe and switched to driving on the right. Momentarily most viewers today believe Borg to be in the wrong when he has his crucial near-collision on the left-hand side of the road with the vicious engineer Alman and his wife.

Borg's first stop is at his family's former summer house beside a lake. When Marianne goes off for a swim (the suggestion is that she wants to wash this old man right out of her tightly knotted hair), Isak is transported back to a summer morning in the 1890s when the Borg family assembled to celebrate the name day of Uncle Aron. The likely year, suggested by the characters' ages, is 1897; the unquestionable date is 1 July, Aron's name day. Bergman no doubt chose the day (at the height of the short wild strawberry season) before choosing the name, so it seems unlikely that Aron has the biblical connotations of Isak and other names in the film. Isak's nine brothers and sisters are there, as well as Olga, his domineering maternal aunt, Aron, his deaf, eccentric paternal uncle, and his cousin Sara. But their parents and the teenage Isak are apparently down at the lake fishing and thus absent from the celebratory breakfast. The 78-year-old Isak – as unseen, privileged eavesdropper – watches his elder brother Sigfrid make clumsy, amorous advances to Sara (Bibi Andersson) as she picks wild strawberries for her uncle's name day party. Sara is semi-engaged to and apparently in love with the reserved, guilt-ridden, studious Isak. But after running in tears from the dining table, having been teased by Borg's twin sisters about Sigfrid, Sara confides in Borg's sympathetic sister Charlotta that he cannot respond to her in a spontaneous manner. We are made aware that she will subsequently jilt him for, and marry, the simple, skittish Sigfrid, who ends up (according to the screenplay, if not the film) occupying the by no means lightweight position of lecturer in Slavonic Languages at Uppsala.

Borg, Bergman suggests, is a spectator, then as now, in the theatre of his own life, neither enriched by coping with family tensions nor succoured by reciprocal family love. He is that significant hero

celebrated in the existential literature of the 1940s and 50s, the alienated figure in the fictions of Dostoevsky, Strindberg, Barbusse, Hesse, Gide, Sartre and Camus that Colin Wilson wrote about in *The Outsider*, his 1956 best-seller that briefly seemed to capture the mood of the mid-1950s before it was brutally consigned to the dustbin of cultural history. As it happens, Bergman's follow-up to the international success of *Wild Strawberries* was to have been an American-financed version of Camus' *La Chute*, a confessional, penitential first-person novel. The project was aborted following the novelist's death in 1960.

During this second disruption of the film's time there is a reference to an earlier period of Swedish history when the Borg family's eldest son hoists above the summer house the flag of the Swedish-Norwegian Union, which came to an end when the two countries went their different ways following the Treaty of Karlstad of 1905. This flashback is of course also our introduction to the film's title, as Borg watches Sara picking wild strawberries for Uncle Aron.

There is a thesis to be written about the way films have been misunderstood around the world through the false, fanciful or plainly invented translations of their titles. The Swedes themselves are great inventors of titles for foreign films (Ford's *The Quiet Man*, for instance, is known as *Hans vilda fru*, 'His Wild Wife') and Bergman is among the sufferers in the English-speaking world. *Gycklarnas afton*, known in Britain as *Sawdust and Tinsel* and in the United States as *The Naked Night*, means 'The Evening of the Clowns'. *Kvinnodröm* (literally 'Women's Dream') was shown outside Sweden as *Dreams* or *Journey into Autumn*. *Ansiktet*, distributed in Britain as *The Face* (a literal translation) was released in America as *The Magician*; and *Nattvardsgästerna*, which simply, and accurately, means 'The Communicants', was given the English title *Winter Light*. *Wild Strawberries* differs only slightly from the Swedish original, but loses the resonance of *Smultronstället*, which means 'The Wild Strawberry Place'.

The Swedes have quite different words for the cultivated strawberry (*jordgubbe*) and the wild strawberry (*smultron*), and the Swedish equivalent of the *Oxford English Dictionary*, the *Svenska Akademiens Ordbok* (published appropriately enough by the University of Lund), devotes several pages to the endless uses of the word *smultron* and the numerous occasions where it occurs in literature. A *smultronställe* is not merely a place where wild strawberries are found, usually around the Swedish midsummer in late June for a brief, much treasured season before the arrival of the more abundant blueberries and wild raspberries. Traditionally each family member lays claim to his or her own wild strawberry patch in childhood and comes to regard it as (the term is inevitable) their own special preserve. In addition to this literal meaning, *smultronställe* has the figurative connotation of a moment in the past to which someone looks back and which they would like to revisit or recapture. For this reason some Swedish writers have evoked James Joyce's epiphanies and Proust's madeleine to suggest the force of the film's title.

In Bergman's movie Borg is returning to just such a moment, which also happens to be an actual wild strawberry patch, and we assume that this was Borg's own special *smultronställe* which has been handed over to, or possessed by, his cousin Sara and is invaded by his brother Sigfrid. Traditionally, in Scandinavian iconography, wild strawberries symbolise innocence and the ephemeral nature of happiness, which is clearly the case when the ballet dancer heroine and her doomed lover pick *smultron* in *Sommarlek* (*Summer Interlude*, 1950), and when Bibi Andersson as Mia, the jester's wife in *The Seventh Seal*, gives a bowl of *smultron* to the Knight. When Bibi Andersson as Sara spills the strawberries in *Wild Strawberries*, this foreshadows a loss of innocence; when later in the film she announces that there are none to be found, this is a prelude to Borg's experience of banishment and emotional exile. Shortly before his death Victor Sjöström received a letter from an elderly Swedish doctor in New York – she had once treated him for a heart condition – telling him of the memories *Wild Strawberries* had brought back, and remarking: 'Thank you for the good strong reminders. There are real strawberry patches – always and everywhere – if only one bends down and looks for them closely.' Significantly, Sjöström placed this letter in his late wife's diary.[8]

When Borg re-enters the present after this first visit to his past, he is challenged by the present-day Sara (also played by Bibi Andersson), a pipe-smoking student in shirt and shorts. She exudes Swedish liberation but professes herself a virgin and, theologically ignorant, believes her biblical namesake to be the wife of Isaac, rather than his mother. She claims that Isak's childhood summer house is on land that now belongs to her father and she jokes about the age of Borg's car. 'It is antique, just like its owner,' he responds, establishing their flirtatious relationship. She cadges a lift from Borg and Marianne, then produces the two male students, Viktor and Anders, with whom she is hitch-hiking to Italy. Viktor is destined for the church, Anders for a career in medicine; they are competing for Sara's affections the way Isak and his brother were for those of her namesake sixty years before. A particular point is made of the fact that the Sara who married Isak's brother is still alive, an elderly widow beyond sentimental reclamation.

Shortly thereafter, rounding a curve, Borg skids to avoid a collision with a Volkswagen Beetle – in those days the most common car in Sweden – being driven on the wrong side of the road. The owner of the badly damaged Beetle, the middle-aged Catholic engineer Sten Alman, blames the crash on the driving of his actress wife Berit, and the couple continue their corrosive, sado-masochistic squabbling when they are given a lift in Borg's Packard, where they sit in the jump-seats with their backs to the three students. The Almans' unconcealed hatred anticipates the flashback to come, involving Borg and *his* wife. Eventually, after Alman (*alleman* is Swedish for 'everyman' or 'everyone') has provoked his wife into striking him, their behaviour becomes intolerable to Marianne, who since the accident has been at the wheel. They evidently make Marianne think of her own future, but she uses the presence of 'the three children' to order them out of the car. They are left disconsolately walking along the road (though in Bergman's screenplay they sink down on the verge 'like two scolded schoolchildren sitting in a corner').

The film's mood changes radically as the party approaches the south-east shore of Sweden's second largest lake, Vättern, where Borg spent his boyhood and where, so we soon learn, he worked for fifteen years as a much loved general practitioner and district health officer. Borg is recognised by Henrik Åkerman (Max von Sydow), a filling station owner, as the doctor who delivered him and his brother into the world back in the 1920s. Henrik will accept no payment for the petrol and announces his intention of naming the child his wife is expecting after Isak. What has transformed this kindly former GP into a cold egoist? Why did he leave this rewarding rural practice to seek a chair in bacteriology in Stockholm, giving up a life among people to scrutinise parasites through a microscope? 'Perhaps I should have remained here,' he says to himself. Watching this scene now, we inevitably note parallels with the career of Pastor Erik Bergman as outlined in his son's screenplay for Bille August's *Best Intentions* (1992), where the troubled hero abandons his social mission in a remote parish in northern Sweden for a fashionable appointment in the capital.

In the next scene Isak luxuriates in the glow of his past reputation as he takes lunch with Marianne and the students in the garden of a restaurant overlooking the lake at Gränna. He engages in a discussion on religion with Anders, the future Lutheran minister, and Viktor, the future doctor, a contest between the rational and the spiritual proposed in deliberately simplistic terms and echoing the argument between the Knight and his Squire in *The Seventh Seal*. Anders, who is idly strumming on his guitar, begins to play the seventeenth-century melody by J. Crüger which is now associated with the words of a hymn composed in 1818 by Johan Olof Wallin (1779–1839), poet, theologian and archbishop, one of the greatest figures in Swedish church history. Anders recites the fifth verse of the hymn, and then Borg takes over, going back to the beginning, and between them he, Marianne and Anders recite the first two verses and the beginning of the third:[9]

Max von Sydow (rt.) as Henrik, the filling station owner

Var är den Vän som överallt jag söker?
När dagen gryr, min längtan blott sig öker;
när dagen flyr, jag än ej honom finner,
fast hjärtat brinner.

[*Where is the Friend I seek where'er I'm going?*
At break of dawn my need for him is growing.
At night he is not there to still my yearning.
My heart is burning.]

Jag ser hans spår varhelst en kraft sig röjer,
En blomma doftar och ett ax sig böjer
Uti den suck jag drar, den luft jag andas
Hans kärlek blandas.

[*I see his footprints here in nature's power*
The weighted wheat that bends, the scented flower.
His love is in the very air I'm breathing,
the sigh I'm heaving.]

Isak taking lunch with Marianne and the students

Jag hör hans röst där sommarvinden susar,
där lunden sjunger, och där floden brusar;
jag hör den ljuvast i mitt hjärta tala
och mig hugsvala.

[*I hear his voice where summer's breezes quiver
through leafy boughs or on the foaming river;
and in my heart it can most sweetly move me;
its balm can soothe me.*]

Ack, när så mycket skönt i varje åder
av skapelsen och livet sig förråder,
hur skön då måste själva källan vara,
den evigt klara!

[*Oh when such beauty everywhere is showing,
in every aspect of creation glowing,
how bright must be the source of this reflection!
What pure perfection!*]

Wallin's verses have an erotic, sensuous undertone, and in addition to the nostalgic yearning induced by the wine taken with his lunch, Borg is both playing on his feelings for the two Saras and touching on the boys' contest over the modern Sara. Viktor, the medical student, remarks: 'As a *love* poem it isn't too bad.'

Isak and Marianne then leave the students, to visit Borg's mother, a 96-year-old widow, at her country house. She is played by the actress and former opera singer Naima Wifstrand (1890–1968), Sjöström's junior by some eleven years. This edgy reunion with her only surviving child is charged with unsentimental thoughts of mortality and decay. The mother is as lonely and isolated as her son. She constantly talks of being cold and we note the link to Isak and Evald. Her failing memory causes her to mistake Marianne for Isak's wife, whom she evidently detested. Isak is treated, and acts, like a child. From the beginning of *Wild Strawberries* (Miss Agda acting as a nanny) to the end (Miss Agda tucking Borg up in bed), a central satiric strategy is of adults being treated as children or seeking to return to the nursery, and of children attempting to act like mature adults.

In the pre-credits sequence, the camera smoothly observes the photographs and artefacts of Borg's well-ordered study. In his mother's house the pictures and family memorabilia are picked up at random from cluttered boxes, ironically commented on, and set aside. Among them is his father's gold watch which his mother proposes giving to a grandchild. Like the clock in Isak's nightmare it has no hands.

As Isak and Marianne leave, his mother alludes to the very summer of the 1890s that Isak revisited in his first flashback. A hint of the new understanding between the Professor and his independent-minded daughter-in-law is clearly announced as they prepare to rejoin the three hitchhikers, but when they continue their journey south with Marianne at the wheel, Isak's reveries and his nightmares merge. A storm is coming on and, agitated by the modern Sara playing off one angry suitor against the other, Isak drifts back into memories of his late-Victorian coming of age. But now the brightly lit morning dream has turned into a sinister twilight of figures silhouetted against a threatening sky. A flock of birds scatters, their wings beating like the angels of death. A basket of wild strawberries has fallen over, scattering its contents on the grass.

Isak with his mother, looking through photographs

Whereas Borg has previously been a benign unseen spectator of his past, Sara now looks directly at him, holds up a mirror to his old, ravaged face (no one ever feels flattered by their mirror image in a Bergman film), and savagely rejects him in favour of his brother, accusing him of emotional frigidity. She next goes to pick up a baby from a cradle on a hill, the child of Isak's married sister Sigbritt in the first dream, but now evidently a symbol of Sara's blissful domesticity, from which Isak is excluded. He finds himself alone, locked outside the family house within which Sara and Sigfrid seem idyllically happy. As he strains to look through the window, his hand accidentally grasps a nail on the wall, producing a wound that we immediately identify with the stigmata of Christ. This symbolically charged scratch suggests (to Borg and to Judaeo-Christian spectators) intense pain, humiliation and the possibility of salvation.

At this point Sten Alman, the Catholic engineer from the motor accident a couple of hours before, appears to lead Borg through the house, now devoid of furniture, and along a bleak corridor to a university examination room. The raked auditorium benches are occupied by ten figures, among them, vaguely to be seen on the front

Sara shows Isak his face in the mirror

bench and formally dressed, Sara, Anders and Viktor. Alman puts him to the test with bacteriological specimens under a microscope (the slides contain nothing); a meaningless text to be read and elucidated; and a corpse to be inspected – Alman's wife Berit, who comes to life and mocks Borg with her laughter. Isak cannot recall, under interrogation, the Hippocratic oath, though in fact what the interrogator is seeking is the admission that a doctor's first duty is to beg for forgiveness. Borg discovers he is 'guilty of guilt'. Kafkaesque or Strindbergian as this trial scene may appear, it is also unnervingly close to the traumatic public inquisition, or *doktorsdisputation*, that Swedish doctoral candidates undergo, and which Borg would have well remembered after fifty years.

Following the examination, Alman leads Borg from the house to a forest clearing where – returning as Alman says to Tuesday, 1 May 1917 – he sees his wife having sex with a sweaty, sensual lover, a scene that echoes the painful sexual humiliations of Frost the clown and Albert the circus proprietor that, respectively, begin and end *Sawdust and Tinsel*. The point is less her infidelity than her belief that Borg will forgive her, magnanimously posing as God Almighty. His compassion, however, is false – it derives from his coldness, his lack of passion.

3 0   Alman (Gunnar Sjöberg) puts Isak to the test

When Borg awakes from this terrible dream, the hitchhikers have left the car to stretch their legs, and Isak remarks to Marianne that in the dream 'I was trying to say something to myself which I don't want to hear when I'm awake . . . That I'm dead, though I live.' At this point Isak and Marianne have a crucial confrontation that leads into the only scene in which Isak does not appear – a rain-drenched flashback in which Marianne and his tormented son Evald (played by Gunnar Björnstrand) drive to the seaside. They step outside their car (a tinny ring as the door closes reveals the inferiority of its make to Borg's substantial American sedan) and discuss their future, most crucially Evald's unpaid debt to his father and her pregnancy. This chilling scene recalls the title of Bergman's second film, an archetypal title of the post-war European art-house cinema, *Det regnar på vår kärlek* (*It Rains on Our Love*, 1946), his first film featuring Gunnar Björnstrand. Bergman does not, in fact, like sunlight, either that of Sweden or of warmer southern climes. His most dedicated American follower, Woody Allen, shares this feeling and goes to immense trouble to shoot scenes in the rain, making New York appear (as he confessed to the Swedish critic and movie-maker Stig Björkman) as rainy a city as London.[10]

Isak 'sees his wife having sex with a sweaty, sensual lover'

When the film returns to the present, there is the pay-off to a succession of incidents involving smoking: Borg first seen confidently puffing on a cigar in his study; Borg asking Marianne not to smoke in the car as it is unfeminine; the late-Victorian Sara noting the seductively corrupt smell of cigar smoke on the breath of Borg's brother; the 1957 Sara smoking her pipe; Borg enjoying his post-prandial cigar beside Lake Vättern; the refusal of Isak's mother to allow smoking in her house. 'If you want to smoke, you may,' Borg says to Marianne, the first explicit sign of his change of heart. (But there are sinister echoes here of the young Oswald being allowed to puff on the pipe of his diseased father in Ibsen's *Ghosts*.) Before anything more can be said they are joined by the teenage trio. Sara gives Isak a bouquet of wild flowers they've picked in the woods to mark his imminent *jubeldoktorat* (Marianne has told them about it while he slept) and she makes a kind, innocent little speech about youth, wisdom and old age.

The film abruptly cuts to Borg's arrival in Lund. The journey is over, we are back within a determining community. A distant public clock chimes four, and Borg's housekeeper, Miss Agda, is there to help him prepare for the solemn ceremony in the cathedral. His son Evald

3 2   Smoking: Isak lights a cigar

coolly welcomes him into his home and soon both are dressed in white tie and tails and marching in the formal procession.

Although we see two other jubilee doctors, they are not identified. Bergman has dropped a scene from his screenplay in which Borg comments on them and the three converse before the ceremony. They are a Professor Emeritus of Roman Law, Carl-Adam Tiger (he is described as a great fighter, and the name echoes that of Bergman's courageous, academically inclined producer, Carl Anders Dymling), and Jakob Hovelius, a former bishop. Isak and Jakob recall youthful discussions about metaphysics, and the bishop remarks: 'As Schopenhauer says somewhere, "Dreams are a kind of lunacy, and lunacy a kind of dream." But life is also supposed to be a kind of dream, isn't it? Draw your own conclusions.'[11]

After the theatrical ceremony in Lund Cathedral with its Latin addresses by the university's public orator, an exhausted Isak retires to bed early, cosseted by Miss Agda. As a token of his change of heart and readiness to alter his life, he suggests to her that they abandon the social practice of a lifetime of addressing each other in the third person and adopt the second person singular, 'du'. It was still customary in the

Isak asks Marianne not to smoke in the car

Sweden of that time for those unequal in age, class or professional status to address each other in the third person, using name and title instead of a pronoun: i.e. never 'you', always 'Miss Agda' and 'Professor' or 'Professor Borg'. (The formal, politely barbed dialogues of *Smiles of a Summer Night* and *Best Intentions* depend on these linguistic conventions for their ironic power and social nuance.) Miss Agda, unwilling to abandon the comfort of the hierarchical world within which she was reared, rejects this as an invitation to an improper intimacy.

When Miss Agda leaves, the students, representatives of a seemingly new Sweden, arrive. But they engage in another traditional formality by serenading Borg beneath his window in a customary Swedish university way. Adopting a sweet, teasingly flirtatious tone, Sara tells him that he's the one she really loves: 'Today, tomorrow, and for ever.'

Isak next attempts a reconciliation with Evald, who is in evening dress to accompany Marianne to the official festivities from which his father has bowed out. Tension noticeably abates between father and son. Evald makes it clear that he and Marianne will remain together.

The ceremony in Lund cathedral

But Isak doesn't get around, as he intends and we expect, to the magnanimous gesture of cancelling the loan that weighs so heavily on Evald. The Hollywood version of this scene would have Evald say, 'You were never there for me', and it would build up to the tearful climactic exchange: 'I love you, son', 'I love you too, Dad.'

There is no such climax here. F. Scott Fitzgerald noted in a letter to John Dos Passos apropos of the conclusion of *The Great Gatsby*: 'I believe it was Ernest Hemingway who developed to me, in conversation, that the dying fall was preferable to the dramatic ending under certain conditions, and I think we both got the germ of the idea from Conrad.' Fitzgerald added, in a letter to Hemingway, 'the purpose of a work of fiction is to appeal to the lingering after-effects in the reader's mind as differing from, say, the purpose of oratory or philosophy which respectively leave people in a fighting or thoughtful mood.'[12] There is something similar in *Wild Strawberries*. After Marianne and Evald leave, Borg slips into his final reverie, a willed dream in which he returns, as he apparently has done before, to that summer's day in 1897. There are no more wild strawberries, Sara tells him, as she leads Isak through the garden to an inlet or cove by a lake. She leaves

Evald (Gunnar Björnstrand) with Isak

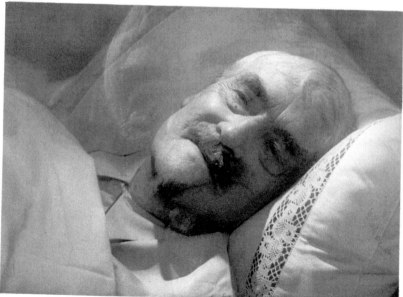

Above: Isak's dream of his mother and father
Below: Isak serene at last

him there as he looks across to where his father is fishing, with his mother sitting beside him. In the first flashback to his childhood, Isak is absent from uncle Aron's name day breakfast, as are his parents. In this final scene we infer that in his mind Isak has detached his relationship with his mother and father from the family and placed it on a superior plane. He calls silently to them and they wave back. In the tableau of this distant vision, Isak has found, or re-created, his *smultronställe*. We cut back via a close-up of the smiling Borg visiting the past to Borg in bed, his expression now serene, in contrast to the troubled countenance with which he awoke from his nightmare that morning.

3
· ·

THE BACKGROUND, THE FOREGROUND

Bergman wrote the screenplay of *Wild Strawberries* in Stockholm's Karolinska Hospital (putative workplace of Isak Borg) in the late spring of 1957 after being given the green light to proceed by Carl Anders Dymling on the basis of a brief scenario. He was in hospital for two months, being treated for his recurrent gastric troubles and general stress, and the chief consultant, Sture Helander, invited him to attend his lectures on psychosomatic illness. Helander, an old friend, was the husband of Gunnel Lindblom, who was to play Isak's sister Charlotta, described in the screenplay as 'the diligent, self-sacrificing sister who carried the responsibilities of the household on her round shoulders'. Bergman was buoyed up by the completion of a triumphant season at the Malmö City Theatre, where he had been artistic director since 1952, and the success of both *Smiles of a Summer Night* and *The Seventh Seal*. But his private life was in disarray: his third marriage was on the rocks; his affair with Bibi Andersson, which had begun in 1954, was coming to an end; his relationship with his parents was, after an attempted reconciliation with his mother, at a desperately low ebb.

For some years Bergman explained the genesis of *Wild Strawberries* as deriving from the experience of visiting his late grandmother's apartment in Uppsala while on a drive from Stockholm to his grandmother's summer house in the province of Dalarna. According to this story he had imagined what it would be like to step back into one's childhood as a fully grown man. From that came the notion of the central character being a doctor, 'a tired, old egocentric, who'd cut himself off from everything around him – as I had done'.[13] Only after writing the script, he claimed, did he think of Victor Sjöström for the role of Borg, and Dymling acted as go-between.

Twenty years later Bergman characterises this version as quite simply a lie. 'The truth is that I am forever living in my childhood, wandering through darkened apartments, strolling through quiet Uppsala streets, standing in front of a summer cottage and listening to the enormous double trunk birch tree.'[14] In this view Isak Borg is both a version of Pastor Erik Bergman, through which the movie-maker attempts to see things from his parents' point of view, and Ingmar Bergman himself, crying out to his mother and father for their love and attention: 'The driving force in *Wild Strawberries* is, therefore, a desperate attempt to justify myself to mythically oversized parents who have turned away, an attempt that was doomed to failure.' He now says that the suggestion for casting Sjöström came from Dymling, 'and as I recall, I thought long and hard before I agreed to let him have the part.'

. . . .

Wild Strawberries went into production within weeks of the completion of the script and was before the cameras from early July to late August 1957. The scenes at the summer house were filmed in Saltsjöbaden, a fashionable resort in the Stockholm archipelago; part of the nightmare sequence with the hearse was shot in the eerie pre-dawn summer light in Gamla Stan, the old part of central Stockholm; but most of the movie was made at SF's studio and on its backlot at Råsunda in northern Stockholm. As the cinematographer Gunnar Fischer recalls, a good deal of back projection was needed:

> Victor Sjöström was very old and ill and very weak. So we couldn't take him out and shoot it in the car. So we had to make every shot with back projection in the studio. And our back projection was not very good and we had no time to make tests. We had to shoot everything so that it would be all right from the very beginning and they were not very good. I hate to see them now.[15]

Actually the back projections are not at all bad, and until the coming of the videocassette we never examined them. We kept intending to look out for them but we were always so closely drawn into the story that we forgot. Truffaut reacted in the same way to the mechanics of *The Lady Vanishes*:

> Since I know it by heart, I tell myself each time that I'm going to ignore the plot, to examine the train and see if it's really moving, or look at the transparencies, or to study the camera movements inside the compartments. But each time I become so absorbed by the characters and the story that I've yet to figure out the mechanics of that film.[16]

Dymling had been unable to secure insurance from Lloyd's of London to cover the production because of the demand for two medical certificates attesting to the star's fitness to undertake so exacting a role. Once the movie was well under way and everyone concerned had come to understand that the project centred on Sjöström, it proved to be what most of the participants recall as an enjoyable and harmonious experience. But there were difficult moments during the first days and a certain tension on the set.

Initially there was trouble over Sjöström's problems with his lines. He would go off into a corner and beat his head against the wall in frustration, even to the point of drawing blood and producing bruises. He sometimes quibbled over details in the script. Ingrid Thulin came to an agreement with Bergman that if anything went wrong in the scenes between Isak Borg and Marianne, she would always take the blame.[17] Much later Bergman came to understand that Sjöström's rages and fractiousness must have stemmed from an old man's feelings that he was no longer up to it.[18] But when it became a routine matter for shooting to end early, so that Sjöström could be home to have his ritual evening whisky at 4.30 p.m., a more relaxed mood was established, though there was a little trouble one afternoon when Sjöström was detained at the studio after 4.30 to catch the particular light needed for the scene where Isak sees his parents by the lake.

A flirtatious relationship grew up between the 22-year-old Bibi Andersson and the 78-year-old ladies' man Sjöström, which is reflected in the tenderness between them on screen. It mitigates a deal of what Andersson considers false in her own playing. With especial warmth

Bergman recalls the way that between takes everyone would gather around Sjöström 'like inquisitive children', questioning him about his early adventures in film-making.

The most bizarre episode during filming was undoubtedly the affair of the snakes – hundreds, possibly thousands by some accounts – that had been kept in a special terrarium in the studio. The intention was that in the second nightmare scene, Borg and Alman should step through a sea of snakes on their way to viewing Borg's wife making adulterous love in the forest. This scene, which Bergman conceived on paper (and which is to be found in his screenplay), might well have provided viewers with a memorable frisson. But it would have proved a crude conjunction between Freudian phallic dreams and the Evil Eden of Judaeo-Christian mythology, so it was probably just as well that in the night before the shooting the reptiles all escaped.

As usual Bergman chose as his collaborators a team of actors and technicians with whom he had worked before in the cinema and the theatre. Once again, his cinematographer was Gunnar Fischer. The spare, unobtrusive score was the eighth of the eleven written for Bergman pictures by the versatile Erik Nordgren.

Music is used sparingly in *Wild Strawberries* and it is combined with heightened natural sounds (a heartbeat, a ticking clock) and the dramatic employment of silence. Only over the credit titles are we made aware of something resembling a traditional film score – an elegiac, slightly baroque composition. Moving into the dream there is a sustained, almost imperceptible and eerie note, redolent of gothic horror. For the most part music in the present-day, realistic scenes has an obvious source – Anders strumming his guitar, Sten Alman aggressively whistling a regimental march, the formal trumpet fanfare in Lund, the students serenading Isak at the end. The rare exceptions occur when certain suggestive motifs are heard over the shot of the handless watch at Isak's mother's house and at the point when Isak becomes a *jubeldoktor* in Lund. Played on harp, cello or celeste, they are picked up from the subtly suggestive music that accompanies the dream sequences.

A film dependent on smooth transitions between studio and location, past and present, dream and reality is helped by having the services of Oscar Rosander, Sweden's finest editor (and incidentally for two years in the early 1950s the chief film editor at the movie-making unit of the United Nations). His association with Bergman had begun on the ill-fated *Crisis* and continued for a further eleven films. Gunnar Björnstrand and Max von Sydow, who had the leading roles in *The Seventh Seal*, here took modest supporting parts, while Ingrid Thulin, who had been in several Bergman productions on the Malmö stage, made the first of her eight appearances in Bergman movies. (Her then husband, the engineer, critic and creator of the Swedish Film Institute, Harry Schein, had blasted Bergman's *To Joy* in his movie column in *Bonniers Litterära Magasin* but later became one of the director's closest friends and has walk-on roles in *The Face* and *The Touch*.) More than a dozen members of the cast had worked with Bergman before or were to work with him again.

Bergman's assistant director was the actor Gösta Ekman, son of the actor-director Hasse Ekman (who appeared in Bergman's *Prison*, *Thirst* and *Sawdust and Tinsel*) and grandson of one of Sweden's greatest actors, also called Gösta Ekman. Back in 1912 the latter had played the lead in Victor Sjöström's directorial debut, *The Gardener* (a film banned in Sweden and thought to have disappeared until a copy surfaced in 1979 in the Library of Congress), and he later played the title role in Murnau's *Faust* (1926).

As noted earlier, Bergman's first wife, Else Fisher, made a brief, uncredited appearance as Borg's mother in the final flashback; their daughter, Lena, played one of Isak's twin sisters.

. . . .

Whether or not Bergman had Sjöström in mind while writing *Wild Strawberries*, Sjöström came to dominate the movie during its production and to become inseparable from our memories and experience of it on the screen. Present in every scene except for the flashback to Marianne and Evald's conversation beside the sea, the 78-year-old actor gives one of the great performances in movie history, an unsurpassed portrait of resilient, rebarbative, unsentimental old age. The film's sixty-year journey into the past and its fifteen-hour one through the present are registered by an endlessly expressive face that exhibits the experience of a lifetime, a subtly modulated old man's voice and a body that learned to speak in silent films. With a tilt of the head, the flick of a muscle, a slight upward vocal inflection, he can reveal the rare emotional depths that his mind and heart are tapping. Such is the power of the performance that it is possible to view Isak Borg not as some kind of emotional cripple in need of sympathy and a spiritual awakening but as a tough proud stoic, capable of taking a critical look at an honourable, inevitably flawed life. This can be seen as introducing a central dramatic contradiction into the film, which was certainly the view of the *New York Times* critic Bosley Crowther: 'He is so real and sensitive and poignant, so winning of sympathy in every way, that Mr Bergman's explanation doesn't make sense.'[19]

Looking back from his own seventies, re-viewing *Wild Strawberries* in his private cinema in Fårö in 1989, Bergman remarks:

> What I had not grasped until now was that Victor Sjöström took my text, made it his own, invested it with his own experiences: his pain, his misanthropy, his brutality, sorrow, fear, loneliness, coldness, warmth, hardness and ennui. Borrowing my father's form, he occupied my soul and made it all his own – *there wasn't even a crumb left over for me!* He did this with the sovereign power and passion of a gargantuan personality. I had nothing to add, not even a sensible or irrational comment. *Wild Strawberries* was no longer my film; it was Victor Sjöström's.[20]

But Sjöström contributed more than his personality. Bergman was steeped in the movies of the man he considered the supreme genius of Swedish cinema.

First of all there are certain stylistic devices that may have influenced Bergman. One thinks especially of the way Sjöström would have within the same shot a succession of receding frames, each a little theatre itself. The audience's attention would be directed down a corridor or through adjoining rooms, without the director cutting or tracking. This is very marked in Sjöström's first masterwork, *Ingeborg Holm* (1913), a powerful story of a decent woman destroyed by a cruel fate and an unfeeling society, which Bergman is not alone in regarding as the true beginning of Swedish cinema.

Then there are possible references to scenes from Sjöström's films. In *Karin, Daughter of Ingmar* (1919), a recurrent motif is a watch without hands, a legacy sought by the hero, which might have influenced the handless time-pieces that occur in Isak Borg's nightmare and at his mother's house. The clock in the nightmare symbolises time having run out, the end of life. It hangs outside a watchmaker and optician's shop over a giant pair of spectacles with staring eyes in the lens, suggestive of both the all-seeing gaze of some cruel deity and a harsh personal interrogation. These glasses are almost certainly a reference to, or inspired by, one of the most famous symbols in twentieth-century literature, the terrifyingly judgmental eyes of Dr T. J. Eckleburg hanging above the oculist's store on Long Island which the characters in Scott Fitzgerald's *The Great Gatsby* pass on their journeys to and from Manhattan. Even the name of Dr Eberhard Isak Borg echoes that of Dr T. J. Eckleburg.

The most obvious debt, however, is to Sjöström's *Körkarlen* (1920), a movie variously known outside Sweden as *Thy Soul Shall Bear Witness*, *The Stroke of Midnight*, *The Phantom Chariot* and (the customary British title) *The Phantom Carriage*. (The literal meaning of the title is 'The Coachman'.) Based on a Selma Lagerlöf novel, it stars Sjöström himself as David Holm, a drunken wastrel (but something too of a holy drinker), who has deserted his wife and family and betrayed the trust of Sister Edith, a Salvation Army officer now dying. While she prays for his soul from her deathbed on New Year's Eve, Holm sits in a graveyard regaling his fellow topers with a ghost story told him by another drop-out. A man who dies at the stroke of midnight on New Year's Eve, he says, becomes the new driver of the phantom carriage that goes around picking up the dead. Suddenly Holm himself is struck down and his soul leaves his body to become a transparent ghost. He is, however, given the opportunity through Sister Edith's devotion to review his life and reconsider his ways. In consequence, Holm is able to keep death at bay, save his wife from suicide, and make a fresh start. It is eventually revealed that Holm had only been knocked out and that the apparently supernatural events we see had been occurring in his subconscious mind.

The film was taken up by temperance organisations and religious groups in Sweden and elsewhere (it was through the offices of Pastor Erik Bergman that Ingmar first saw *The Phantom Carriage*). But its psychological sophistication and its respect for Holm's bloody-minded independence temper the didacticism. Technically it remains impressive (Julius Jaenzon's photography and double-exposure special effects are remarkable), and its complicated structure of flashbacks within flashbacks was innovatory in its day and anticipates *Wild Strawberries*. In her book *Flashbacks in Film*, Maureen Turim remarks on its 'use of a cinematic means of expression for this ambivalence between states of dreaming, premonition, remembering, and the supernatural', and she makes considerable claims for the seminal contributions to the development of the flashback by both Sjöström and Stiller.[21]

Anyone who has thought of a possible link between the mid-20th-century summer's day of Isak Borg and the mid-19th-century Christmas Eve of Ebenezer Scrooge will be pleased to have this confirmed by the letters of Selma Lagerlöf published in 1992. Writing to her friend Sophie Elkan in August 1912, she says: 'For years I have carried around in my head a plan to write one of those short Christmas stories that Dickens used to write ...' And only a week later: 'If I could only finish my *Christmas Carol*, 90 to 100 pages or so, I would bring it out as a separate small volume before Christmas.'[22] The book is of course *Körkarlen*, which finally appeared in 1912 and forms the middle link in the chain between *Christmas Carol* (1843) and *Wild Strawberries* (1957). Bergman has often expressed his admiration for *Körkarlen*. He owns a copy of the film and apparently sees it at least once a year. The hearse of which David Holm is designated the new driver anticipates the nightmare that changes Isak Borg's plans, and the final line of Lagerlöf's novel (which is also the final intertitle of Sjöström's film) could well serve as the epigraph to *Wild Strawberries*: '*Gud, låt min själ få komma till mognad, innan den ska skördas!*' (God, let my soul reach maturity before the reaper cuts it down!).

. . . .

Bergman first came across the plays of August Strindberg at the age of twelve, and he was overwhelmed: 'Quite simply, I copied Strindberg. I tried to write like him, dialogues, scenes, everything. Without comparison Strindberg was my idol. His vitality, his anger, I felt it all within me. I believe I wrote quite a few Strindberg-inspired plays.'[23] The playwright lies everywhere behind the film-maker's work and the two men shared a lifelong fascination with magic lanterns. While we might consider *The Hour of the Wolf* or *Scenes from a Marriage* to reflect very strongly different aspects of Strindberg, the perceptive French critic N. T. Bihn has called *Wild Strawberries* 'le film le plus "Strindbergien" de Bergman'.[24] He has a case.

To Damascus (1898) and, even more so, *A Dream Play* (1901) dissolve the gap between dream and reality, and the latter, which is Bergman's favourite Strindberg work, anticipates a number of incidents in *Wild Strawberries*. It may well be that they insinuated themselves into the screenplay because Bergman had not at that time realised his ambition of staging the play; this he was to do three times, most notably the 1970 production in the Dramaten's small studio theatre with scarcely any decor and a cast of twenty-four, which was presented in the International Theatre season in London the following year.

There is in *A Dream Play* a reference to a childhood memory of an unhappy experience being made up for with a bowl of wild strawberries. There is also a nightmarish examination in which the Officer finds himself, despite having a doctorate, back in a schoolroom being humiliated by a sadistic examiner. A lawyer, a philosopher, a theologian and a doctor engage in a simplistic debate like the one pursued by the students Viktor and Anders. A key scene centres upon an elaborate award ceremony at a university that, as Michael Meyer points out in the introduction to his translation of Bergman's adaptation of *A Dream Play*, probably derived from a false rumour which had reached Strindberg the previous year that Lund was to confer on him an honorary doctorate.[25] Evald's debt to his father in *Wild Strawberries* echoes the comment of *A Dream Play*'s lawyer: 'They get married early, earning 2,000 crowns when they need 4,000 crowns; so they borrow, everybody borrows money until they die.'

Appalling accounts of embattled married couples held together by erotic desire and sado-masochistic urges while tearing each other apart are so frequent in Strindberg as to be considered his special territory – one thinks especially of *The Father* and *The Dance of Death*. Similar marriages are to be found in *Wild Strawberries*: Isak Borg's shown in flashback, that of the engineer Sten Alman and his wife Berit, who – like two of Strindberg's wives – is an actress. Alman, responding to Marianne's scolding of him for baiting his wife, remarks: 'This is my way of enduring. I ridicule my wife and she ridicules me. She has her hysterics and I have my Catholicism. But we need each other's company. It's only out of pure selfishness that we haven't murdered each other by now.' This is very close to the words of the Mummy (played by Naima Wifstrand in Bergman's 1954 Malmö production) in Strindberg's *The Ghost Sonata*. 'Crimes and guilt and secrets bind us together, do you understand? Our ties have been broken and we have gone our different ways so many times, but we are always drawn together again.'[26] There is a further echo from *The Ghost Sonata* in the concern throughout *Wild Strawberries* with ticking clocks, sudden silences, time stopping. 'I can stop time in its course. I can annihilate the past,' the Mummy says. 'I can make what is done undone. But not through bribes, nor menaces, but through suffering and repentance.'[27] In Strindberg's published text, the Mummy puts her hands over the clock before speaking. In Bergman's production script from 1954, the Mummy does not step over to the clock and silence time until she has said, 'I can make what is done undone.'[28]

The disgusting Alman and his oppressed wife were based on Stig Ahlgren, the scathing movie critic of the influential mass-circulation weekly magazine *Vecko-Journalen*, and his wife Birgit Tengroth, a celebrated actress and author, who not only appeared in Bergman's *Thirst* (also known as *My Three Loves*, 1949) but also wrote the short story on which it was based. (Alman's Catholicism may be a reference to Herbert Grevenius, the critic and screenwriter on several Bergman films, including *Thirst*, whose close friendship with Bergman foundered following Grevenius's conversion to Rome.) The actors were cast because of their resemblance to the director's targets. Bergman explained his attack by saying that 'Stig Ahlgren had just beheaded me for something or other, and this was my revenge'; he subsequently regretted the petty malice involved, but Ahlgren seems to have been unaffected.[29] Three years later he accused *Through a Glass Darkly* of bringing out latent schizophrenia in the viewer.[30]

Strindberg often lampooned ex-friends and opponents in his work, and when Bergman fired off a broadside at his traducers in the Stockholm tabloid press before going into exile, he quoted a remark of Strindberg's: 'Watch out, you bastard, I'll see you in my next play.' In his sixty-fifth and final play, *Stora Landsvägen* (*The Great Highway*, 1909), Strindberg viciously laid into several contemporaries by way of easily identifiable caricatures. He subtitled *The Great Highway* '*Ett Vandringsdrama med Sju Stationer*' ('a travelling play with seven stations'), which to modern ears suggests a road movie on the way to Calvary. This highly autobiographical play centres on an allegorical journey by an ageing figure called The Hunter (*Jägarn*), who revisits key scenes and places in his life as he prepares to die, meeting a variety of emblematic figures. It has rarely been revived since its premiere in

1909 at Strindberg's own, 161-seat Intimate Theatre in Stockholm. (It was dutifully presented at the Dramaten in Stockholm in 1949 to mark the centenary of Strindberg's birth, with Lars Hanson – star of Sjöström's *The Wind* – as The Hunter, and in late 1993 it was given a triumphant British premiere at the minute Gate Theatre, Notting Hill, in a vigorous translation by Kenneth McLeish.) It was evidently on Bergman's mind, though, while he was making *Wild Strawberries*.

In February 1960 Bergman delivered an address at the memorial celebration arranged by the Swedish Film Academy to mark the death of Victor Sjöström at the age of eighty on 3 January 1960. Bergman, who had drafted Sjöström's 1944 tribute to Kaj Munk, expressed himself lost for words.[31] 'No. I can't compose a speech in memory of Victor Sjöström,' he began. 'I suspect he would smile with the utmost irony if he could see me making such a speech.' Instead he read some jottings from the diary he had kept during the making of *Wild Strawberries*, and he concluded with his observations of Sjöström's face, shot in close-up 'in a dirty studio' for the final moments of the movie:

> This exceedingly shy human being would never have shown us lookers-on this deeply buried treasure of a sensitive purity, if it had not been a piece of acting: in simulation ...
>
> In the presence of this face I recalled the final words of Strindberg's last drama *The Great Highway*, the prayer to a god somewhere in the darkness.
>
> 'Bless me, Thy humanity
> That suffers, suffers from Thy gift of life!
> Me first, who most have suffered –
> Suffered most the pain of not being what I most would be.'
>
> [*Välsigna mig, din mänsklighet,
> som lider, lider av din livsens gåva!
> Mig först, som lidit mest –
> som lidit mest av smärtan
> att icke kunna vara den jag ville!*]

Bergman has made several television versions of Strindberg. He has never adapted him for the screen, though Alf Sjöberg, who directed Bergman's first screenplay, made three movie versions, one of them – *Miss Julie* – a masterpiece. *A Dream Play* was originally thought unstageable, but five years after its publication it was produced in Germany. Bergman declared it unfilmable, but in 1994 a Norwegian director, Unni Straume, in deliberate defiance of this dictum, made a black-and-white movie version of the play, set in present-day Oslo and starring three of Bergman's key actors – Erland Josephson, Bibi Andersson and Liv Ullmann. A cinema, where Ullmann works in the box office and where movie star Andersson's films are screened, is one of the movie's chief settings. Unni Straume's ambitious *Drømspel* cannot be said to have proved Bergman wrong. Strindberg was himself a gifted photographer and passionately interested in the cinema. Like Selma Lagerlöf, he was keen to see his work filmed, and movie versions of two of his plays were made in the year of his death (1912).

. . . .

Bergman is often quoted to the effect that the theatre is his wife and the cinema his mistress, and a man who has had five of one and a dozen of the other knows whereof he speaks. According to his reliable biographer Peter Cowie, what he actually said back in 1950 is: 'The theatre is like a loyal wife, film is a great adventure, the costly and demanding mistress – you worship both, each in its own way.' He has also said: 'There has always been a short distance between my work in the theatre and my work in the film studio. Sometimes this has been an advantage and sometimes a burden, but the distance has always been small.'[32] It is in fact most enlightening to look at the plays he was engaged on immediately before embarking on *Wild Strawberries* and the one he was thinking of while writing it.

The first play he directed in the 1956–7 season at Malmö (it opened on 1 October 1956) was the Swedish premiere of Tennessee Williams' *Cat on a Hot Tin Roof*, a play first staged on Broadway in 1955 and first presented in Britain under club conditions in 1958 after being refused a licence from the Lord Chamberlain for public performance because of its references to homosexuality. Williams' play foreshadows themes and relationships in Bergman's film and in its published form carries as an epigraph the final stanza of Dylan Thomas's angry poem directed to his old dying father, 'Do not go gentle into that good night'. The opening of this stanza – 'And you, my father, there on the sad height,/Curse, bless me now with your fierce tears, I pray' – would have had a special meaning for Bergman; it is possibly a reference to Søren

Kierkegaard's discovery that his father once stood on a hill and cursed God.

Like *Wild Strawberries*, *Cat on a Hot Tin Roof* centres on the relationship between an overbearing father, a withdrawn, emotionally crippled grown-up son, and a vital, combative daughter-in-law. They're Big Daddy (in Bergman's production, Benkt-Åke Benktsson, the fat fashion tycoon in *Journey into Autumn*, the tavern-keeper in *The Seventh Seal*), a rich landowner in the Deep South, his embittered son Brick (Max von Sydow), who's financially dependent on him, and Brick's wife Maggie (Eva Stiberg). The play takes place over a single day during which Big Daddy, afflicted with terminal cancer, is confronting his imminent death. Maggie, who wishes to have a child by the cold, sexually ambivalent Brick (and thus ensure his inheritance), has a crucial scene with her father-in-law, in which she claims that she is pregnant, and ends up forcing a tentative reconciliation on her husband. The view of death that Big Daddy expresses to Brick – 'When you're gone from here, boy, you are long gone, and no where' – is one that Bergman, the agnostic son of the manse, would probably endorse.

His second production that season (premiered on 7 December 1956) was Strindberg's *Erik XIV* (1899), starring Toivo Pawlo (the police chief in *The Face*) as the doomed sixteenth-century Swedish king whose plans to marry Queen Elizabeth of England are thwarted, and his life eventually ruined, by his love for the commoner Karin Månsdotter (Bibi Andersson). The play has been called Sweden's *Hamlet* and it had been filmed in 1954 (as *Karin Månsdotter*) by Alf Sjöberg, featuring Jarl Kulle and Ulla Jacobsson (both to have leading roles in *Smiles of a Summer Night* the following year) and photographed in colour by Sven Nykvist, who was to succeed Gunnar Fischer as Bergman's regular director of photography. The remote, tortured aristocrat reaching out to an ordinary woman of the people expressed a powerful urge within Strindberg; Isak Borg would appear to have similar feelings. The play contains a celebrated Strindberg line: '*Nej mitt barn, livets strider ta aldrig slut*' ('No, my child, the struggles of life never end').

Bergman's final production of the season was Ibsen's *Peer Gynt*, which opened on 8 March 1957, a matter of days before he booked into the Karolinska hospital, and its cast included ten actors who were to appear in *Wild Strawberries*: Max von Sydow in the title role, Gunnel Lindblom as Solveig, Ingrid Thulin as Anitra, Åke Fridell as the

Mountain King, Naima Wifstrand as Mother Åse, and Bibi Andersson, Jullan Kindahl, Björn Bjelvenstam, Maud Hansson and Yngve Nordwall. Ibsen's verse drama, published in 1867 and first performed in 1876, influenced *A Dream Play* and was the model for *The Great Highway*. The play covers some sixty years, and Peer's flight from home and from himself, with its variety of amusing and sometimes horrific encounters in Norway and Africa (a life's compromised journeying that brings him back home to the lost love of his youth and a confrontation with death), is a phantasmagoric blueprint for *Wild Strawberries*.

The fourth play is Molière's *The Misanthrope*, which Bergman had in mind for the following season, and his production did in fact open in Malmö on 6 December 1957, a couple of weeks before the premiere of *Wild Strawberries*. Max von Sydow played Alceste, and while making *Wild Strawberries* Bergman must have had in mind this proud, detached man, disdainful of human weakness and incapable of hypocrisy, who is yet caught up in an impossible love affair with the passionate, wilful, coquettish Célimène. It is significant that on the Malmö stage Célimène was played by Gertrud Fridh, who has the part of Borg's spirited, unfaithful wife in *Wild Strawberries*. Several theatre reviewers compared von Sydow's Alceste with Jimmy Porter, the archetypal 'angry young man' anti-hero of John Osborne's *Look Back in Anger* (1956).

Another play that seems to lie behind *Wild Strawberries* is *Death of a Salesman*. Bergman in fact never directed it, nor indeed anything else by Arthur Miller, though (naive as it may sound today) it was a critical commonplace in the 1950s to talk of Tennessee Williams as the American Chekhov and Miller as the American Ibsen. The way that Miller's tragic travelling salesman, Willy Loman, slips into and out of his past, always remaining his middle-aged self while in these sometimes pleasant, sometimes agonising reveries, resembles the experience of Isak Borg. As it happens, Victor Sjöström was among the first European actors to play Willy Loman in a 1949 production at the Municipal Theatre of Norrköping. At the age of seventy, he was almost certainly the oldest actor to take on the taxing role that the 37-year-old Lee J. Cobb had created on Broadway earlier that year. Sjöström's performance was universally acclaimed. Herbert Grevenius (1901–93), at the time one of Bergman's regular collaborators and in Bergman's view 'one of the best theatre critics Sweden ever had', dropped a note to Sjöström immediately after seeing his Norrköping Willy Loman:

Dear Mr Sjöström,

Was at the theatre last night. Am so moved I scarcely know how
to express my gratitude and admiration. I must have been really
immune to the play. It is the fifth time I have seen it, and in four
versions, but not until now has it gripped me so completely.

Yours,

Herbert Grevenius

It is inconceivable that Bergman did not hear about this performance.
But if he did not think of *Death of a Salesman* while making *Wild
Strawberries*, Victor Sjöström surely did.

....

Wild Strawberries interweaves what might broadly be called
Expressionism with a realistic depiction of the romantic, haunting light
of the Swedish summer. The only scene not set in a nightmare limbo or
in the summer months is the flashback when we first meet Evald and
Marianne tells him of her pregnancy. She specifically describes it as
taking place 'a few months ago', i.e. in March, and the scene is shot in
the bleak grey style of Bergman's movies of the 1940s.

Borg's reveries or flashbacks, whatever one wishes to call them,
transport him to his youth in the 1890s and the film's visual style is
much influenced by, and at times specifically involves, the work of the
two most celebrated Scandinavian artists, the Norwegian Edvard
Munch (1863–1944) and the Swede Carl Larsson (1853–1919), both as
popular today as they were at the turn of the century. They were close
friends of Strindberg and they produced the most famous portraits of
him: Munch's (dated 1896 and famously misspelling the playwright's
name as 'Stindberg') makes him appear dishevelled and demonic;
Larsson's (dated 1899) presents him as dapper and dandyish.

Comparing their large and immensely varied *oeuvres*, which reflect
the major currents of late nineteenth-century European painting,
Scandinavian folk art and the new influences from the Orient, especially
Japan, the two men are closer to each other than is generally supposed.
Likewise they are nearer in character than the popular perception of a
neurotic, alienated Munch and an ebullient, uxorious Larsson would

have us believe. It is, however, what we think of as most characteristic of their work of the 1890s that *Wild Strawberries* reflects – and this may well be an essential dichotomy in the manic-depressive Scandinavian character that explains why Bergman's movies (like much Scandinavian art) so often enact the prelude to tragedy but end up tentatively affirmative in tone.

Larsson is best known for the pictures celebrating the apparent domestic bliss of his country household at Sundborn in the province of Dalarna, not far from the summer home of Bergman's maternal grandmother. The most popular works from this period (reproductions hang in the hallways of most Swedish homes and on the walls of supermarkets) are the twenty-six watercolours called *Ett hem* (A Home). They show a large, happy, modestly affluent family throughout the year, enjoying themselves according to each season. The overall lighting of these pictures, with scarcely a shadow to be seen, unites a new reading of Scandinavian light with Japanese art. The austerely elegant, pale furnishings of Larsson's domestic interiors, so different from prevailing Victorian tastes for the dark, heavy and ornate, reflect

Carl Larsson, *Ett Hem: Skamvran* (*The Punishment Corner*) (1890)

his reclamation of the traditional Swedish styles as part of the National Romantic Movement, and his admiration for William Morris's 'arts and crafts' movement and the work of the Scottish designer Charles Rennie Mackintosh.[35] These Larsson paintings were less descriptive than prescriptive, less a realistic depiction of his own life than an ideal, 'a model for those who feel a need to furnish their homes agreeably'. What he was creating was a national dream.[36] They helped influence the direction Swedish interior decoration and domestic architecture took for well over half a century, almost wholly for the good. They made taste a social issue, and contributed to raising aesthetic judgments to the level of cultural imperatives.

The first flashback to the family gathering at the Borgs' summer home in the 1890s is designed and lit in the manner of Larsson and such followers of his as Fanny Brate and Anna Anckarcrona. (Brate's most famous painting, executed in 1902 and a perennial best-seller as a postcard, is called *Namnsdagsuppvaktning*, 'Name day celebration'.) The furniture is identical and the white suits and dresses are designed to cast no shadows. Likewise when Isak Borg has his final memory of his

The flashback to the family gathering

mother and father fishing beside the lake at the end of *Wild Strawberries*, we return to the idyllic Larsson world. A quarter of a century later, in *Fanny and Alexander*, Bergman and Sven Nykvist luxuriantly re-created the world of Carl Larsson in carefully graded colour and artfully contrived compositions. This may well be one of the reasons that Scandinavian audiences finally took Bergman to their hearts in 1982.

The darker side of Scandinavia was being explored in the 1890s by Edvard Munch when he too was developing an individual style. Strindberg wrote an essay for *La Revue Blanche* on the occasion of Munch's exhibition at the gallery L'Art Nouveau in Paris, and you could substitute the name Strindberg or Bergman for that of Munch in the opening paragraph:

> Edvard Munch, aged 32, the esoteric painter of love, jealousy, death and sadness, has often been the victim of the deliberate misrepresentations of the executioner-critic who does his work with detachment and, like the public executioner, receives so much per head.
>
> He has come to Paris to be understood by the initiate, with no fear of the mockery which destroys cowards and weaklings but which, like a shaft of sunlight, lends a new brilliance to the shield of the valiant.[37]

If the opening nightmare of *Wild Strawberries* owes anything to Munch it is the notion of terror taking place in the summer night that offers no escape into darkness. But visually this scene comes from a later development of Expressionism, the tradition of cinematic dreams that reaches down from German silent movies like Robert Wiene's *The Cabinet of Dr Caligari* (1919) and G. W. Pabst's *Secrets of a Soul* (1926) through to the Hollywood *film noir* of the 1940s. The most famous American example is, of course, Hitchcock's *Spellbound* (1945), which Bergman had certainly seen, but there are also such domestic uses as Spencer Tracy's wedding-eve nightmare in Vincente Minnelli's *Father of the Bride* (1950), which is quite as terrifying as Borg's. It is possible that the portmanteau Ealing anthology of macabre stories, *Dead of Night* (1945), which among other things features a dream of a horse-drawn hearse in broad daylight, had some influence.

The first obvious reference to Munch comes when Borg enters

the old family summer house and stands to the right of the frame as the Larsson-like preparations for breakfast go on inside. This shot draws on the series of Munch paintings from the 1890s (which Strindberg was reviewing in Paris) in which the foreground figure has his or her back to the other people, though they are manifestly very much on, or in, his or her mind. The figure is lonely, agonised, detached, and we read the painting starting from the foreground. This scene of Borg imaging, or imagining, his past, closely resembles Munch's *Jealousy* (1895), one of Strindberg's favourite paintings. In *Jealousy*, a distraught husband or lover, dressed in black and looking both straight ahead and into himself, stands in the foreground to the right of the canvas. In the background is a sinister re-enactment of the temptation of Adam by Eve, her red dress open to reveal her naked body as she plucks an apple for the man beside her. In *Wild Strawberries* this account of the Fall is replaced by an Edenic scene from Larsson.

Later, in the second return-to-childhood dream, Munch takes over almost entirely in the earlier part. When Borg stands outside the house, excluded from the apparent domestic bliss of his brother and Sara, this is pure Munch. The evident source of this image is the painting (1893) and woodcut (1895) called *Moonlight*, wherein a peculiarly poignant woman stands outside a wooden house at night. When Borg views his wife's infidelity, we return to something resembling *Jealousy*.

What is noticeable throughout *Wild Strawberries* is the way Borg nearly always retains his dark overcoat, which detaches him from the background in the manner of a Munch figure. Also, as with Munch's men and women of the 1890s, he is frequently presented with his back to people, most obviously when he is in the front seat of the car, driving. On these occasions, of course, what is going on in the background, as he can see in the rearview mirror, is a repetition of the relationship between his brother, himself and the 'historic' Sara, and a re-enactment by the Almans of scenes from his own marriage. When he has his longest conversation with his son, Evald himself has his back to Borg.

It is possible that there may be a reference to Munch much earlier on, though this could be simply *ben trovato*. The scene following the opening nightmare when the worried Borg comes to the bedroom of Miss Agda, his housekeeper, has an astonishing likeness to Munch's

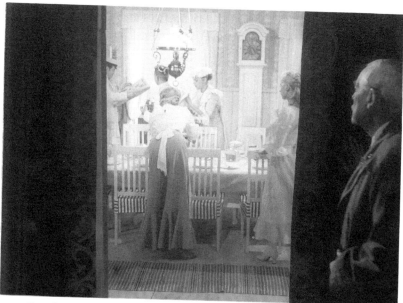

Above: Edvard Munch, *Jealousy* (1895)

Below: Isak, detached and lonely, observing the family scene

1942 self-portrait, painted during the German occupation of Norway, when he was 78, the same age as Isak Borg. Both Borg and Munch are framed in a doorway, their scrawny, uncovered necks vulnerable, their shoulders round, with a grandfather clock behind them as well as a closed door in the rear and pictures on the wall. There is certainly a marked physical resemblance between these proud, lonely, elderly men.

What may also be a coincidence, though it seems unlikely, is the evocation of Munch in the original Svensk Filmindustri poster for *Wild Strawberries*. The dominant colour is a shade of blue, or actually bands of blue, associated with Munch – as in one of his most famous paintings, *The Dance of Life* (1899–1900), where the sea and sky merge in the background of a summer night. (Munch's Danish contemporary, P. S. Krøyer, also went in for this particular effect of the 'blue hour'.) The photograph of Victor Sjöström that dominates the composition is given a grainy look which closely resembles the characteristic texture – almost a signature – of the innovative coloured woodcuts that Edvard Munch began to make in the mid-1890s.

4
. . . .
THE TIMES, THE REPUTATION

Wild Strawberries was Ingmar Bergman's return to the contemporary world after two movies in historical settings: *Smiles of a Summer Night* takes place at the turn of the century, *The Seventh Seal* in the Middle Ages. Only one of his next three pictures (the obstetric drama *So Close to Life*, written by Ulla Isaksson) is set in the present. *The Face* (his only original screenplay between 1957 and 1961) is located in mid-19th-century Stockholm, and *The Virgin Spring* (also written by Ulla Isaksson) in mediaeval Sweden. His central character in *Wild Strawberries* is of course a hangover from an older society, and clearly part of Bergman's intention at a social level is to compare Borg, the creation of a repressed, late-Victorian middle-class world, with the children of the new, supposedly liberated Sweden where the Permissive Society (a British coinage of the following decade) was born. Rarely thereafter was Bergman to deal directly with everyday life in contemporary Sweden. Only a handful of his later movies are about people with commonplace occupations and preoccupations – *So Close to*

Life, The Devil's Eye, Winter Light, Scenes from a Marriage, Face to Face and *Autumn Sonata* – and in most of these the leading characters are priests, the wives of priests, and psychotherapists.

Jörn Donner, one of Bergman's most perceptive early critics and himself a film-maker, in writing of *Wild Strawberries*, remarks on Strindberg and Bergman as emerging 'during two separate epochs of crisis in the Swedish community'.[38] Strindberg 'interprets the changes from the breakthrough of capitalism to the victory of democracy'. He wrote as Sweden was being transformed from a backward, rural society to a progressive urban one, with Stockholm turning into a sophisticated capital city. Donner sees him as a man torn between 'aristocratic and democratic ideals' and struggling to reconcile these conflicting impulses. Bergman, making *Wild Strawberries* exactly fifty years after the production of Strindberg's final play, is looking at Sweden following a quarter of a century of Social Democratic rule. The Social Democrats came to power after a bitter period of social unrest. A series of major strikes had culminated in a bloody encounter between trade unionists, blacklegs and the army in a northern industrial community that left five strikers dead, an event commemorated in Bo Widerberg's film *Ådalen 31* (1969).

During the nineteenth century more than a quarter of the Swedish population had emigrated from a backward, impoverished country, mostly to the United States. But by the 1950s the Social Democrats (who as the dominant element in a wartime coalition government kept the country neutral during World War II) had brought an unprecedented prosperity to Sweden and created the world's most advanced welfare state. The nation was run by bureaucrats, technocrats and social scientists. Trade union leaders and captains of industry were in constant contact with the government and with each other so that social and industrial problems were confronted in a rational manner on the basis of a widespread national consensus. Although Lutheran Protestantism remained the official state religion (it still is), the church's influence had waned and attendance fallen drastically. Conformity was accompanied by a considerable degree of freedom in matters of artistic expression and sexual conduct. While alcohol could be bought only from uninviting, aseptic off-licence shops, the *systembolaget* run by the state (liquor had actually been rationed from 1919 until the mid-1950s), contraceptive advice was readily available to teenagers throughout the country. Sweden seemed to have passed beyond poverty and politics, certainly beyond contesting ideologies, and to have reached a point where the only worthwhile issues left to be considered were of an aesthetic, ethical and spiritual nature, and the only unanswered questions eschatological ones.

For some time foreign observers, including those disillusioned with the prospects for the future offered by both the Soviet Union and the United States, had been turning to Sweden as a guide to the prospect before mankind. From their visits they returned with stories that were variously lubricious, encouraging and alarming. In the late 1930s the American liberal journalist Marquis W. Childs had written the laudatory *Sweden: The Middle Way*, which he updated in 1948, confirming his original views. The *Time* magazine reporter Joe David Brown (who was also a Southern Baptist and novelist whose book *Addie Pray* was the source of Peter Bogdanovich's film *Paper Moon*) came back from a Scandinavian trip with a different, more sensational report, one consonant with the country's reputation that was building in the United States and around the world as a result of *One Summer of Happiness*. Because of its lyrical nude-bathing sequence (followed by discreet lakeside love-making), Arne Mattsson's delicate tale of a doomed summer love was sold to ninety countries. Brown's 1953 piece, the first occasion that *Time* gave a byline to a staff writer, was called 'Sin and Sweden' and was largely devoted to Swedish materialism, nude bathing, free love, birth control and, inevitably, suicide. In 1960 the British writer Kathleen Nott wrote a scathing book on the sterility and conformity of Sweden, borrowing her title, *A Clean Well Lighted Place*, from the Ernest Hemingway short story. At the same time President Dwight Eisenhower, as the somewhat torpid era that bears his name was drawing to its close, made an official apology after suggesting (or rather, after one of his speech-writers had suggested) that socialism, as evidenced by Sweden, inevitably led to demoralisation, immorality and mass suicide. (As it happens, Sweden and the other Scandinavian countries were just more honest in bringing in suicide verdicts and compiling national statistics. Hungary had a far higher suicide rate, as did the London borough of Hampstead.) Much of the high-mindedness of Sweden of this period was embodied in the aloof, patrician style of the world's number one diplomat, the then Secretary-General of the United Nations, Dag Hammarskjöld.

'As an artist,' Jörn Donner remarks, 'Bergman becomes extraordinarily representative of the change, a victim of the time and simultaneously its interpreter.' In a manner that Donner could not have foreseen, Bergman became the literal victim of the new state. In the middle of his rehearsals of Strindberg's *Dance of Death* in 1976, a pair of plainclothes policemen acting on behalf of the inland revenue department arrested him at the Royal Dramatic Theatre on what were subsequently established as wholly false charges of tax evasion. The result of this Kafkaesque experience was a serious mental and physical breakdown and five years of voluntary exile.

Certainly in the late 1950s the perceived international image of Sweden – at once lewd and dour, liberated and depressed – was the glass through which foreigners darkly saw Bergman's movies. He himself is dismissively critical of the very part of *Wild Strawberries* that touches most realistically on the current scene – his depiction of the three students: 'What is stone dead in *Wild Strawberries* – as far as I now remember it – is the three youngsters. Not the one played by Bibi in the flashbacks: she's rather a sweet girl. But these three are supposed to represent modern kids. Even at that time the image was utterly dated.'[39] He puts his finger on the film's chief weakness. These three are types, seen from the outside. Their idiom rings untrue, as indeed does much of the dialogue put into teenage mouths in movies of the 1950s. Bibi Andersson was twenty-two at the time and as Bergman's lover she was both his chief contact with youth and somewhat removed from the teenage world. She agrees with his verdict on the modern Sara:

> I don't like myself in that film, I think I was doing very clichéd work. I don't know why I made her so superficial. You see, at the time we had so many 'ingénue' roles, and it was like I was acting young. When I did *The Seventh Seal* I was more innocent as an actor. I just sat there and made the thoughts.[40]

Bergman's embarrassment over this aspect of the movie may well be what deterred him from panoramic examinations of a society he knew less than intimately and from further engagement with modern youth, at least in its teenage form. He was happier dealing with children not closely identified with the mores of an evolving society, as in *Through a Glass Darkly*, *The Silence* and, especially, *Fanny and Alexander*.

Bergman's emergence on the international scene was sudden and dramatic. Much more so than most people now recall. David Hare, for instance, in *Plenty*, first staged at the National Theatre in 1978 and filmed by Fred Schepisi in 1985, has the guests at a fashionable London diplomatic cocktail party in October 1956 discussing 'the new Bergman film at the Everyman' as Britain prepares to invade Egypt during the Suez crisis. As it happens, Bergman was little known in 1956 even to dedicated British movie buffs (the term 'movie buff' had yet to cross the Atlantic) and indeed it was not until the autumn of 1958 that the Everyman, Hampstead, Britain's oldest repertory cinema, put on its first Bergman season, consisting of a mere four films: *Sawdust and Tinsel*, *Smiles of a Summer Night* and *The Seventh Seal*, plus Sjöberg's *Frenzy*.

In fact before 1956 only two Bergman movies had been released in Britain. The first was his anti-Communist oddity, *Sånt händer inte här* (*It Can't Happen Here*, 1950), shown in 1953, dubbed into English, cut from eighty-five minutes to sixty-seven, called *High Treason*, and dismissed by the *Monthly Film Bulletin* as 'a confused Swedish contribution to the current "anti-Red" cycle'.[41] The second, *Sawdust and Tinsel*, was released in 1955 in a somewhat censored version and described in the *Monthly Film Bulletin* as 'flashy and rather self-consciously arty' and put down for its 'total lack of humour'.[42]

Bergman had struggled with Dymling to make *Smiles of a Summer Night* and was rewarded first by box-office success in Sweden and then at the 1956 Cannes Festival, where a jury presided over by the imperious French novelist Louise de Vilmorin was evenly divided between giving the main prize to his movie or to Satyajit Ray's *Pather Panchali*. They compromised by awarding the Palme d'Or to the Jacques Cousteau–Louis Malle underwater documentary *Le monde du silence*, and invented a 'Poetic Humour Prize' to honour Bergman and a 'Human Document Prize' for Ray. This success and the immediate overseas sales proved enough to secure a go-ahead for *The Seventh Seal* (on a thirty-five day schedule and the small budget of about £75,000). British recognition, however, was less than immediate. Lindsay Anderson, who in 1988 was to narrate the second part of Thames Television's two-hour Bergman documentary for Channel 4 and to talk of the way Bergman transformed international cinema, covered the Cannes Festival for *Sight and Sound*. His eight-page report did not mention *Smiles of a Summer Night*. By the next issue of the magazine

(Autumn 1956) the movie had opened in London but was only accorded a single star in the quarterly guide to current releases and was faintly praised by John Gillett in the 'In Brief' section: 'On the evidence of his past work, he is clearly a director of considerable technical fluency and invention. But despite the glimpses of pity and affection in his latest film, the prevailing mood remains defiantly cynical and jaundiced.'

The following year, *The Seventh Seal* shared the Special Jury Prize at Cannes with Andrzej Wajda's *Kanal*, and it opened later that year around the world to near universal acclaim. It was one of those seemingly esoteric works – *Waiting for Godot* is another from the same period – that reverberate in a way that causes them to impinge on the consciousness of those who haven't seen them and will probably never see them. The expectations for *Wild Strawberries* were immoderately high when it opened on 26 December 1957 at the Röda Kvarn, the same Stockholm cinema where Sjöström's *The Phantom Carriage* had its premiere on New Year's Day 1921. (Röda Kvarn – *moulin rouge* – was the name Bergman gave his magic lantern cinema in his nursery.) It went on to win the Golden Bear and ecstatic reviews from the international press at the Berlin Festival in February 1958. Two months later, *So Close to Life* (which Bergman had shot rapidly in late 1957 in order to fulfil a longstanding obligation to Nordisk Tonefilm, after staging *The Misanthrope* in Malmö) won prizes at Cannes for best director and for best actress (awarded jointly to its four leading ladies). In 1959 *Wild Strawberries* brought Bergman his first Oscar nomination. It was short-listed in the category 'Best Story and Screenplay written directly for the screen' along with *Les Quatre cents coups, North by Northwest*, Blake Edwards' *Operation Petticoat* and the Doris Day–Rock Hudson vehicle *Pillow Talk*. It was the only film written entirely by its director (François Truffaut shared a credit with Marcel Moussy for *Les Quatre cents coups*), but the members of the Academy of Motion Picture Arts and Sciences decided to honour the four Hollywood writers responsible for *Pillow Talk*. The following year, however, Bergman received the Best Foreign Language Film Oscar for *The Virgin Spring*.

We, the authors of this monograph, regard *Wild Strawberries* as one of the best films ever made, a film that can stand comparison with the greatest works of art from any era. We think it a complex, ambiguous, richly suggestive film. We do not, however, find it obscure or unduly problematic, as are a good many Bergman films of the following two decades. But *Wild Strawberries* was almost universally considered a difficult and demanding picture when it first appeared. Bosley Crowther, for example, the long-standing movie critic of the *New York Times*, to whom the silent films of Victor Sjöström were no earlier than yesterday afternoon, wrote:

> If any of you thought you had trouble understanding what Ingmar Bergman was trying to convey in his beautiful poetic and allegorical Swedish film *The Seventh Seal*, wait until you see his *Wild Strawberries* which came to the Beekman yesterday. This one is so thoroughly mystifying that we wonder whether Mr Bergman himself knows what he was trying to say.[43]

The British newspaper reviewers wrote favourably of both *The Seventh Seal* and *Wild Strawberries* when they opened in, respectively, the spring and autumn of 1958. But for some the admiration was accompanied by repulsion. Dilys Powell, for instance, in the *Sunday Times* welcomed *The Seventh Seal* as 'a notable film', but after praising its technical excellence and noting its allegorical power, she laid about the movie in a ferocious manner, concluding:

> Death playing chess on the sea-shore – it would be consoling to be able to say that the magniloquent symbols conceal something bogus as well as sentimental. But they don't; Mr Bergman, I am sure, has a midnight, Arctic-winter sincerity; the violence of my dislike of his film is probably evidence of that. Did I say *The Seventh Seal* was sobering? On me it has the impact of one of those spiked iron balls chained to a club, so popular in films about goodwill in the Middle Ages.[44]

The British Film Institute's *Monthly Film Bulletin* remained cautious and lukewarm. Of *The Seventh Seal*, 'JM' (presumably John Minchinton) wrote: 'It is difficult to follow what Bergman is saying, because he has no clear statement to make ... Nevertheless the film is full of beautiful images and powerful atmosphere.'[45] The same journal's review of *Wild Strawberries* – written by 'KC', presumably the classical scholar Kenneth Cavander, who wrote a similar piece for its quarterly companion *Sight and Sound* – was even less enthusiastic. After criticising the film's 'tantalising portentousness', he went on to observe that the religious symbolism provided clues 'so elusive that they distract, rather than focus attention. They certainly do not cohere, and the final impression left by the film is of the work of a man obsessed by cruelty, especially spiritual cruelty, trying to find some resolution.'[46] Dilys Powell's sister critic, and longtime Sunday rival, C. A. Lejeune, movie reviewer of the *Observer* from 1929 to 1960, opined:

> In the past, Bergman's films have often been inclined to wrath; *Wild Strawberries* is merciful … [It] could have been a desperately sentimental film. It isn't. It could have been ragged and perplexing. It isn't. Magnificently but very quietly played, in the grand style, by Victor Sjöström, the first of the great Swedish directors, it mixes dream, memory and actuality so smoothly that one is only aware, at the end of it, of life as a continuing thing that touches, takes, releases and then passes on.[47]

Bergman was a man whose time had come. The leaders of the British intelligentsia had stumbled in seizing on Colin Wilson and his *The Outsider* in 1956 as the author and seminal work our troubled society needed. The cult of the Angry Young Man had run its course. In the confused post-Suez, post-Hungarian Revolution mood of Western Europe here was a practising artist engaging with the key issues of the day, working simultaneously in the elite art of the theatre and the popular medium of the cinema, yet situated observantly on the fringe of the polarised East-West, Cold War confrontation. It is not easy in the 1990s to recapture either what Sweden meant in a cultural sense or the peculiar status suddenly conferred on Bergman. Everyone, from Michael Frayn in the *Manchester Guardian* to Lionel Trilling in *The Mid-Century*, was writing about him.

In 1959 Bergman's newest film, *The Face*, opened in London, and five early films were given their first public screenings in Britain – *Summer with Monika* (1953), *A Lesson in Love* (1954), *Journey into Autumn* (1954), *Port of Call* (1948) and *Summer Interlude* (1950). The following year *Waiting Women* (1952) finally reached Britain, and in 1961 four Bergman pictures were released – *Night is My Future* (1947), *The Devil's Wanton* (or *Prison*, 1949), and two recent productions, *So Close to Life*

(1958) and *The Virgin Spring* (1959). In 1962 came the first film in the chamber trilogy, *Through a Glass Darkly* (1961), and in 1963 there was *The Devil's Eye* (1960) and the second film of the chamber trilogy, *Winter Light* (1963), the only Bergman film to open in Britain the same year it was given its premiere in Sweden. Bergman's burgeoning international reputation culminated in his appearance in spring 1960 on the cover of *Time*, then America's most authoritative magazine and among the most influential in the world. In a lengthy cover story essay he was embraced in characteristic fashion by a journal still very much under the sway of its founder, Henry Luce, the patrician Republican who had been born in China, the son of a Presbyterian missionary:

> The Bergman boom fits into the cultural context of the times. His is a voice crying in the midst of prosperity that man cannot live by prosperity alone. Turning from the troubled scene around him – 'I have no social conscience,' he has said – Bergman has focused his lens on the interior landscape, and his work emerges as an allegory on the progress of the soul – his own, and by inference the soul of modern man. He is a Bunyan in show business, a religious artist whose glimpses of the dark side of man are without equal in the history of the cinema.[48]

But did this international reputation help at home? As far as his producers were concerned it did. For the first time in years they were handling a director (as opposed to a single film like *One Summer of Happiness*) in worldwide demand. Nonetheless, to secure the modest budget for *The Virgin Spring*, Bergman had to agree to follow it up immediately with the bright sex comedy *The Devil's Eye*. As is so often the case, it was the difficult art-house movie that proved the money-spinner and the safe commercial picture that flopped.

As far as Swedish critics were concerned, however, one must take into consideration that odd phenomenon, *den kungliga svenska avundsjukan* (the royal Swedish envy), which serves to cut down Swedes who achieve international success. Both Garbo, to a certain extent (a typical article in the January 1933 number of *Vecko-Journalen*, the weekly paper for which Bergman's antagonist Stig Ahlgren was later to write, compared her Hollywood career unfavourably with Dietrich's), and Ingrid Bergman, to a considerable degree, suffered thus. Not to mention more vulnerable people such as Anita Ekberg and Maj Britt.

The generous critical reception that from the start greeted Bergman's work in the theatre was not matched by the national movie reviewers. They noted his talent but took a long while to acclaim his films. He lacked a significant advocate, and the often disparaging attitude of local intellectuals to his screenplays led to him refusing invitations to publish them in Swedish, though he authorised a 1960 American translation of *Smiles of a Summer Night*, *The Seventh Seal*, *Wild Strawberries* and *The Face*. (There is still no Swedish version of these texts.) His first film book in Swedish, published in 1963, was *En filmtrilogi*, his highly literary scenarios for *Through a Glass Darkly*, *Winter Light* and *The Silence*.

Of *Smiles of a Summer Night* the critic in the right-wing evening tabloid *Expressen* wrote: 'The main story about the young wife who is still a virgin seems forced. Altogether the single-minded concentration on this side of human life makes the irritating impression on the spectator that the author/director suffers from a case of delayed puberty.' In the review in the liberal morning broadsheet *Dagens Nyheter*, Bergman is warned against using the same actors time and again. The situation was little changed for *The Seventh Seal*. Again in *Dagens Nyheter*, the reviewer professes that he did not share the director's interest in the problem of good versus evil and says that 'Ingmar Bergman's direction this time – and not just this time – is superior to his script.' Marianne Höök in the conservative morning broadsheet *Svenska Dagbladet* is entirely enthusiastic: 'Has ever a more beautiful film been made in this country – or anywhere?' But the Social Democrat evening tabloid *Aftonbladet* calls it 'an elegant question mark'. When *Wild Strawberries* opened less than a year later, the *Dagens Nyheter* critic, Carl Björkman, finds that 'the film lacks intrinsic spontaneity' but gratefully acknowledges 'its many exquisite human and artistic qualities'. The pseudonymous 'Lill' (Ellen Lilliedahl) in *Svenska Dagbladet* admires the film without reservation and ends her review by saying that it 'must surely win over those people with any feeling for film who are still resistant to Bergman'. Staffan Tjerneld in *Expressen* praises the actors, in particular Sjöström, Jullan Kindahl (Miss Agda) and Ingrid Thulin, finding

only one failure in the production and that is Bergman the writer, who has been enticed to provide a script for Bergman the director but has had little of his own to add. He has just delivered various literary borrowings. ... As the maker of *Wild Strawberries* has serious pretentions, the shortcomings of the film's content is a serious matter.

In the early 1960s books on Bergman began to appear in Sweden. (Naturally the first book on him was in French: Jean Béranger's *Ingmar Bergman et ses films*, 1960.) The first two Swedish books devoted entirely to his films, by Marianne Höök and Jörn Donner, were generally admiring in their tone. The third, ostensibly about the state of Scandinavian cinema, by the future film-maker Bo Widerberg, was something of a frontal attack on Bergman. Widerberg's *The Vision of Swedish Film* (1962) might well be compared with Pauline Kael's *I Lost It at the Movies*, published three years later. Both were assaults on the critical, film-making and production establishments of national cultural capitals by combative critics living in proud, provincial cities, in her case San Francisco, in his Malmö.

Widerberg was dismissive of all Swedish film-makers except for Sjöberg, Sucksdorff and Bergman, though he thought all three had gone astray. He demanded the creation of a film culture that could inspire movies which were as formally innovative and responsive to contemporary life as those of the French *nouvelle vague*. Widerberg argued that Bergman's international success was something of a barrier to bringing this about. 'Bergman,' he wrote, 'meets halfway the very coarsest myths of ourselves and what is ours, underlines the misconceptions that foreigners love to retain.' He spoke of Bergman as 'our painted Dalecarlia horse to the world', a man remote from the genuine concerns of the Sweden of the time. After comparing *Wild Strawberries* unfavourably with two other outstanding movies featuring lonely, elderly, dying men, Kurosawa's *Ikiru* (1952) and Vittorio De Sica's *Umberto D* (1952), he commented: 'a lost God, a lost wild strawberry place, a lost summer is obviously a theme on which to make a film. But I think this private nostalgia, if it becomes a genre, is fatal for the growth of Swedish film.'[49] In the films he himself was to make in the 1960s Widerberg substituted for this private nostalgia a public nostalgia that harked back to a harsher, crueller, more socially divided Sweden.

Those years in the late 1950s and early 60s when Bergman

emerged on the international scene were among the most vital and significant in the history of cinema. Still hampered by severe censorship, caught up in the confusion attendant upon the declining influence of the big studios in the face of competition from television and the legally enforced sale under anti-trust legislation of their chains of cinemas, Hollywood was in a mood that was both conservative and indecisive. As the Eisenhower era gave way to the short-lived Kennedy years, a demand for change was everywhere in the air. A new generation of film-makers emerged on the scene, born like John Kennedy in this century and, in most cases, since World War I. Fellini, Visconti, Antonioni, Rosi and Pasolini from Italy; Ray from India; Bergman from Sweden; Wajda from Poland; Kurosawa, Mizoguchi (who had died in 1956 while being discovered in the West) and Ozu from Japan; Luis Buñuel, returning from Mexico to the international scene and his European roots; Tony Richardson, Karel Reisz, Lindsay Anderson and the Free Cinema Movement linking criticism and movie-making in Britain; Malle, Chabrol, Truffaut, Godard and the French critics turned film-makers who launched the *nouvelle vague.*

There was a feeling abroad that film had come of age. That a mature international cinema was on the point of replacing industrial Hollywood. That a generation had arrived that could make movies as fluently as they might once have written novels. That there was a large, worldwide audience for movies innovative in form, personal in character, moral, philosophical and political in thrust, intellectually playful and deeply serious in tone.

Things did not quite turn out that way. A new generation of film-makers and critics, acting initially under the influence of the writing (principally for *Cahiers du cinéma*) of the French New Wave and their leading American ally, Andrew Sarris, rediscovered Hollywood and moved in to take it over. The American industry attained a new respectability just as its history was being written. This was accompanied by a major shift in the sensibility of a large section of the educated class throughout the English-speaking world as a result of the validation of popular culture as a proper subject for study and a widespread challenge to (almost an onslaught on) traditional cultural values and criteria.

Certainly after the early 1960s Bergman ceased to excite fashionable audiences and fire the young as he had once done. This does not mean that his later work was not respected, or that following the dip in his reputation after the indifferent films made during his period of exile in Bavaria during the late 1970s he was not everywhere revered as a master. But his status is neatly, if condescendingly, summed up by Richard Corliss, the *Time* magazine reviewer who in 1991 greeted the award of the Palme d'Or at Cannes to a US film for the third year running as a sign of the American cinema's permanent superiority:

> Back then we all took ourselves, the cinema and Bergman much more seriously. Bergman's solemnity, his insularity, his *largo* pacing, his insistence that viewers work for their pleasure, all are aspects of a temperament foreign in every way to the passionate profligacy of the new Hollywood technocrats. When Bergman is cited in a movie these days, it is in a mixed spirit of homage and parody; and it comes from film-makers (Woody Allen, Monty Python) working from an older sensibility, one that grew up with a sub-title squint in the eye and the linger of cappuccino in the nostrils.[50]

Wild Strawberries has taken a permanent place in the classic repertoire of world cinema (in 1972 it sneaked in at ninth place – equal with Mizoguchi's *Ugetsu Monogatari* – in the international poll of the ten best films of all time taken every decade by *Sight and Sound*, though it subsequently dropped several places). It has also proved influential in two ways. The first is that along with Alain Resnais' *Hiroshima mon amour* it created a new relationship in the cinema between external and internal reality, a new concept of cinematic time that Bergman and Resnais were themselves to develop over the next decade and which was to affect permanently the way films have since been made and understood. Dennis Potter (1935–94), arguably the most important television dramatist to have emerged in Britain, brought their ideas and perceptions to a mass audience on the small screen. It would be wrong to say they invented something. What we are talking about is a point when film-makers and audiences became conscious of a significant change, and their movies made us and make us consider in a new way the writers and film-makers of the past to whom Bergman and Resnais were indebted. This is what Jorge Luis Borges meant when he said that 'each writer *creates* his precursors. His work modifies our conception of the past, as it will modify the future.'

The second long-term effect was the key role *Wild Strawberries* played in creating what from the late 1960s was to become a major cinematic genre, the road movie. This is thought of as an American form, connected to the size and rawness of North America, and the peculiar transaction between its citizens – still, if only figuratively, the sons and daughters of pioneers – and the land. Indeed there is a case for seeing the pivotal American novel of the 19th century, *The Adventures of Huckleberry Finn*, as anticipating the genre.

But what *Wild Strawberries* did so decisively was to bring to the movies and the motor car that symbolic, allegorical rendering of life as a didactic journey that had been such a key feature of mediaeval literature. One thinks especially of the English morality play *Everyman*, of Dante's *La Divina Commedia* ('Halfway along the road that is our life I found myself in a dark wood where the straight way was lost'), and also of that atavistic masterpiece of the 17th century, John Bunyan's *The Pilgrim's Progress*. This earlier form was revived by Expressionist and Symbolist artists, both writers and painters, reacting against the prevailing realistic tradition towards the end of the 19th century. It was through them that the allegorical journey was mediated to Bergman, especially via Ibsen's *Peer Gynt* and Strindberg's *To Damascus*, *The Dream Play* and *The Great Highway*. Egil Törnqvist, however, sees a more direct line from Dante, suggesting that the initial nightmare, the second flashback to the 1890s (the one that includes the interrogation) and the final reverie correspond respectively to his *Inferno*, *Purgatorio* and *Paradiso*.[51] Törnqvist also proposes a parallel between Borg's journey and the Stations of the Cross, one of them being the filling station managed by Max von Sydow, though he doesn't point out that seven years later von Sydow played Christ in George Stevens's *The Greatest Story Ever Told*.

In *Images*, Bergman calls *The Seventh Seal* 'a sort of road movie', using the English term in his Swedish text ('blev en sorts *road movie*').[52] He thus modestly places the film in a genre that did not then officially exist, and suggests that his link in the cultural chain went straight back to the Middle Ages by way of his actors' rehearsal piece and radio play *Trämålning* (*A Picture Painted on Wood*, 1954), which was inspired by mediaeval allegorical paintings in Swedish churches. *The Seventh Seal* does have essential elements of the road movie – a protagonist revisiting his past, encountering bizarre representatives of his society along the way and emerging in some manner transformed.

But the real ur-road movie is *Wild Strawberries*, though it could be said that a contribution was also made to the creation of the genre by Rossellini's *Viaggio in Italia* (1953) and Fellini's *La Strada* (1954). The latter incidentally bears the influence of Sjöström. From them flow Francis Ford Coppola's *The Rain People* (1969), Dennis Hopper's *Easy Rider* (1969), Bob Rafelson's *Five Easy Pieces* (1970), Monte Hellman's *Two-Lane Blacktop* (1971), and endless lesser American pictures. In the mid-1970s, Wim Wenders named his Munich-based production company Road Movies, and made a trilogy of road movies – *Alice in the Cities*, *Wrong Movement* and, most famously, *Kings of the Road*. Meanwhile, Joseph Strick's 1973 film about a pair of independent American truckers and their affair with an itinerant prostitute, having flopped in Britain as *Janice*, was released as *Road Movie* in the United States, where it also failed. A decade later Wenders came to Cannes with his American road movie, *Paris, Texas*, and won the Palme d'Or.

The chess game between the knight, Antonius Block, and Death, and the silhouetted Dance of Death on the horizon have become iconic images of our time, making *The Seventh Seal* part of shared popular culture. The most recent, most expensive, least witty reference involved Ian McKellen standing in for Bengt Ekerot as Death. Sir Ian was paid several times the total budget of *The Seventh Seal* to step out of an unlikely revival of Bergman's film at a Times Square cinema in New York for a brief encounter with Arnold Schwarzenegger, playing another fugitive from the world of celluloid, in *The Last Action Hero* (1993), an extravagant Hollywood exercise in Beverly Hills post-modernism. Images of this sort from *Wild Strawberries* have not entered the general consciousness. The title, however, stirs memories whenever and wherever wild strawberries are served. And the film is often quoted – intertextually, as we now say – in other movies. In Gilbert Cates's Bergmanesque *Summer Wishes, Winter Dreams* (1973), the distressed menopausal heroine, Joanne Woodward, sees *Wild Strawberries* at a Greenwich Village art house and it triggers off her own nightmares. Subsequently she revisits her childhood haunts in a manner reminiscent of Isak Borg, and she accompanies her husband on a sentimental journey to the European battlefield where he fought in World War II.

The original screenplay was by the knowing Stewart Stern, author of such *Zeitgeist* films as Nicholas Ray's *Rebel Without a Cause*, Paul Newman's *Rachel, Rachel* and Dennis Hopper's *The Last Movie*; and the title, *Summer Wishes, Winter Dreams*, is a wistful conflation of several Bergman titles.

Twenty years later Bergman's film turns up in Alessandro Di Robilant's *Il Giudice Ragazzino* (*The Law of Courage*, 1993), an admirable contribution to a cycle of angry Italian pictures about brave magistrates putting their lives on the line while prosecuting the Mafia in Sicily. The hero, an idealistic young public prosecutor, meets his future fiancée at a party. She too is a lawyer and her father has been killed by the Mafia, but she will later confront her lover in court as a disinterested, highly paid counsel for accused mafiosi. Has he any other interests apart from the law, she asks. The cinema, he says. This too is her extra-legal passion. So instead of heading for the bedroom, they drive to a cinema in Agrigento. And what do they see? The opening nightmare sequence of *Wild Strawberries* in which Isak Borg foresees his own death. *The Law of Courage*, based on a true story, ends with the assassination of the young lawyer as he drives along a Sicilian road in 1991. The movie is quoted more obliquely in André Téchiné's *Ma Saison préférée* (1993) where the relationships between two French generations resemble those in *Wild Strawberries*. Téchiné came to the cinema after teaching film at IDHEC (he was fifteen when *Les Fraises sauvages* opened in Paris) and his characters, one of them a screwed up doctor, make a journey by car with an elderly parent through evocative childhood places. The 45-year-old heroine (Catherine Deneuve) has a flashback in which she revisits as an adult her now dead mother and father as they sit idyllically fishing on a riverbank, an epiphanous moment when she was four and they were much less than her present age. *Ma Saison préférée* ends with Deneuve reciting in French the hymn by Archbishop Wallin that Borg, Marianne and Anders recollect in *Wild Strawberries*.

The most extensive use of *Wild Strawberries*, however, is to be found in Woody Allen's *Another Woman* (1988). Allen's references to Bergman begin in *Love and Death* (1975), though that film is far more indebted to Bob Hope. *Interiors* (1978), his first non-comedy and his first movie in which he does not appear, is generally regarded as his most Bergmanesque. But *Another Woman* is in effect an extended homage to, and a sort of William Burroughs-style cut-up version of, Bergman's film. In his first collaboration with Bergman's cinematographer Sven Nykvist, Allen confronts his own dual crisis of turning fifty and becoming a father for the first time by putting the film's female narrator, a middle-aged Professor of Philosophy at a New York university who is married to a brain surgeon, through a healing, revealing ordeal similar to Isak Borg's. Called Marion and impersonated by a tightly coiffured Gena Rowlands, she has a striking resemblance to Ingrid Thulin's Marianne in *Wild Strawberries*. Films starring Allen almost invariably take place in a vibrantly Jewish New York; those he merely writes and directs are set in a subdued, pastel-coloured WASP Manhattan, a tasteful Stockholm-on-the-Hudson.

The opening and closing scenes of *Wild Strawberries* and *Another Woman* are almost identical. At the beginning Marion sits at her desk complacently describing her successful career as the camera pans over photographs of relatives we are soon to meet. At the end she reaches for and finds a sudden epiphanous serenity that confirms the discovery of a new understanding of herself. In between, over a handful of painful autumnal days in Manhattan, she experiences a series of dreams, nightmares and disturbing encounters that force her to reassess her life and character. Marion comes to appreciate that she has sacrificed feeling to ambition, cut herself off from everyday humanity, betrayed her professional calling, and in the process become cold and alienated. As with Isak Borg, the judgments made on her by herself and others seem overly harsh.

In a fractured and refracted form, virtually every scene and character from *Wild Strawberries* turns up in Marion's journey into herself and through her past. Her elderly father (played by John Houseman, a cultural figure as old, distinguished and distinctive as Victor Sjöström) gives her a box of family memorabilia that transports her to childhood memories both idyllic and troubled. Echoing Borg's revivifying meeting with the filling station owner (Max von Sydow) whom he had brought into the world, Marion is buttonholed at a restaurant by an admiring former pupil who claims that twenty years ago her life was transformed by a lecture Marion gave on 'Ethics and Moral Responsibility'. A teenager (Marion's stepdaughter) asks awkward questions. Marion, who has refused to make loans to her prodigal brother and his wife, seeks a reconciliation with them. Bergman's dialogue is paraphrased and redistributed among the cast.

There is an explicit reference to Edvard Munch (his *Death and the Maiden* is juxtaposed with Klimt's *Hope* in an emblematic antique shop where Marion has a mystical meeting), but Munch's role as avatar of existential loneliness in *Wild Strawberries* is replaced in Allen's film by evocations of paintings by Edward Hopper. *Another Woman* may not be in the same class as *Wild Strawberries*, but it takes on a new clarity and acquires a greater stature when viewed as a Manhattan reworking of Bergman's masterpiece.

. . . .

In 1970 an experiment was conducted by Dr Christopher Evans of the National Physical Laboratory. He was investigating a theory about dreaming and computer programme clearance. With the collaboration of the editors of the weekend magazine of a British quality newspaper, he submitted to its readers a questionnaire which had as its sole object to find out what films reminded them of their personal dreams.[53] To Evans's surprise, more than 30,000 people returned his questionnaire. It clearly touched them in a vulnerable psychic area, and from their replies over a hundred films emerged. The top fifteen were: 1) Alain Resnais' *L'Année dernière à Marienbad* (1961); 2) Stanley Kubrick's *2001, A Space Odyssey* (1968); 3) Fellini's *Juliet of the Spirits* (1965); 4) Jonathan Miller's television film *Alice in Wonderland* (1966); 5) Bergman's *Wild Strawberries* (1957); 6) George Dunning's *Yellow Submarine* (1968); 7) Fellini's *8½* (1962); 8) Orson Welles's *The Trial* (1962); 9) Antonioni's *Blow-Up* (1966); 10) Jean Cocteau's *Orphée* (1949); 11) David Lean's *Doctor Zhivago* (1965); 12) Robert Enrico's *La rivière du hibou* (*An Incident at Owl Creek*, 1962); 13) Roman Polanski's *Repulsion* (1965); 14) Luis Buñuel's *Belle de jour* (1967); 15) Bergman's *The Seventh Seal* (1957).

Numerous theatres have been named after actors and impresarios. There is even a Broadway theatre named for a drama critic – the Brooks Atkinson. A couple of London cinemas – the Lumière and the Renoir – commemorate French directors. The affectionate titles of several movies allude to their cinematic settings – Basil Dearden's *The Smallest Show on Earth* (1957), Peter Bogdanovich's *The Last Picture Show* (1971), and Giuseppe Tornatore's *Nuovo Cinema Paradiso* (1989). In 1961, however, a Stockholm cinema was renamed *Smultronstället*, the first cinema, so far as we know, to be called after a film. It opened with a Bergman retrospective. Sadly, it is no more, having changed its name after a few years to Puck (presumably considered a less recherché sylvan symbol than wild strawberries), and then moved to another site. But for many moviegoers around the world the favourite picture palace of their childhood is likely to be a personal *smultronställe*.

NOTES

....

1 *Motion Picture Classic*, vol. 19, no. 2, April 1924.
2 Bengt Forslund, *Victor Sjöström* (New York: Zoetrope, 1988), p. 252.
3 Ibid., pp. 256, 263.
4 Ingmar Bergman, *The Magic Lantern*, trans. Joan Tate (London: Hamish Hamilton, 1988), p. 68.
5 Peter Cowie, *Ingmar Bergman: A Critical Biography* (London: Secker & Warburg, 1982), p. 79.
6 Michael Meyer, *Strindberg: A Biography* (London: Secker & Warburg, 1985), p. 231.
7 Ingmar Bergman, *Wild Strawberries* (London: Lorrimer, 1986), p. 24.
8 Forslund, *Victor Sjöström*, p. 265.
9 English translation by Kersti French.
10 *Woody Allen on Woody Allen*, ed. Stig Björkman (London: Faber and Faber, 1994), p. 186.
11 Bergman, *Wild Strawberries* (screenplay), p. 89.
12 *The Letters of F. Scott Fitzgerald*, ed. Andrew Turnbull (London: Bodley Head, 1964), pp. 363, 309.
13 *Bergman on Bergman*, trans. Paul Britten Austin (London: Secker & Warburg, 1973), p. 133.
14 Ingmar Bergman, *Images*, trans. Marianne Ruuth (London: Bloomsbury, 1994), p. 22.
15 *Working with Ingmar Bergman*, ed. Paul Gerhardt, Derek Jones, Edward Buscombe (London: Thames Television/Channel 4/ British Film Institute, 1988), p. 16.
16 *Truffaut on Hitchcock* (London: Secker & Warburg, 1968), p. 95.
17 Bergman, *The Magic Lantern*, pp. 181–2.
18 Forslund, *Victor Sjöström*, p. 267.

19 Bosley Crowther, *New York Times*, 2 June 1959.
20 Bergman, *Images*, p. 24.
21 Maureen Turim, *Flashbacks in Film* (New York and London: Routledge, 1989), pp. 94–8.
22 *Du lär mig att bli fri: Selma Lagerlöf skriver till Sophie Elkan* (Selma Lagerlöf's letters to Sophie Elkan), ed. Ying Toijer-Nilsson (Stockholm: Bonniers, 1992), pp 381–2.
23 Stig Björkman, Olivier Assayas, *Tre dagar med Bergman* (Stockholm: Filmkonst, 1992), p. 14; published as *Conversations avec Bergman* by *Cahiers du cinéma* (1990).
24 N. T. Binh, *Ingmar Bergman, Le magicien du Nord* (Paris: Gallimard, 1993), p. 87.
25 August Strindberg, *A Dream Play* (London: Secker & Warburg, 1973), p. xii.
26 August Strindberg, *Skrifter*, XII (Stockholm: Bonniers, 1955), p. 337.
27 Ibid., p. 340.
28 Lise-Lone and Frederick Marker, *Ingmar Bergman: Four Decades in the Theater* (New York: Cambridge University Press, 1982), p. 73.
29 *Bergman on Bergman*, p. 140.
30 Ibid., p. 130.
31 *Sight and Sound*, Spring 1960, p. 98.
32 Cowie, *Ingmar Bergman*, p. 167.
33 Marker, *Ingmar Bergman*, p. 1.
34 Forslund, *Victor Sjöström*, p. 259.
35 Jocasta Innes, *Scandinavian Painted Decor* (London: Cassell, 1990), pp. 57–9.
36 *Dreams of a Summer Night: Scandinavian Painting at the Turn of the Century* (catalogue for exhibition at the Hayward Gallery, London, 10 July–5 October 1986; Arts Council of Great Britain), p. 176.

37 Thomas Messer, *Munch* (London: Thames & Hudson, 1987), p. 31.

38 Jörn Donner, *The Films of Ingmar Bergman* (New York: Dover, 1972), pp. 154–5.

39 *Bergman on Bergman*, p. 147.

40 *Working with Ingmar Bergman*, p. 32.

41 *Monthly Film Bulletin*, no. 228, January 1953, p. 9.

42 *Monthly Film Bulletin*, no. 257, June 1955, p. 83.

43 Crowther, *New York Times*, 2 June 1959.

44 *The Dilys Powell Film Reader*, ed. Christopher Cook (Manchester: Carcanet, 1991), p. 122.

45 *Monthly Film Bulletin*, no. 292, May 1958, p. 59.

46 *Monthly Film Bulletin*, no. 299, December 1958, p. 151.

47 *The C.A. Lejeune Film Reader*, ed. Anthony Lejeune (Manchester: Carcanet, 1991), p. 299.

48 *Time*, 14 March 1960, pp. 14ff.

49 Bo Widerberg, *Visionen i svensk film* (Stockholm: Bonniers, 1962), p. 31.

50 Richard Corliss, *Foreign Affairs*, ed. Kathy Schulz-Huffhines (San Francisco: Mercury House, 1991), p. 108.

51 Egil Törnqvist, *Filmdiktaren Ingmar Bergman* (Stockholm: Arena, 1993), p. 43.

52 Bergman, *Images*, p. 232.

53 Basil Wright, *The Long View* (London: Secker & Warburg, 1974), pp. 13–14.

CREDITS

· ·

Wild Strawberries (Smultronstället)

Sweden
1957
Production Company
Svensk Filmindustri (SF)
Swedish premiere
26 December 1957
UK release
1958
UK distributor
Gala Films
Production manager
Allan Ekelund
Director
Ingmar Bergman
Assistant director
Gösta Ekman
Screenplay
Ingmar Bergman
Photography (black and white)
Gunnar Fischer
Assistant cameraman
Björn Thermenius
Music
Erik Nordgren
Musical direction
E. Eckert-Lundin
Editor
Oscar Rosander
Art direction
Gittan Gustafsson
Costumes
Millie Ström
Make-up
Nils Nittel (of Carl M. Lundh)
Sound
Aaby Wedin, Lennart Wallin
Production buyer
Karl-Arne Bergman
Unit manager
Sven Sjönell
Scriptgirl
Katherina Faragó
91 minutes
2,490 metres

Victor Sjöström
Professor Isak Borg
Naima Wifstrand
Borg's mother
Jullan Kindahl
Miss Agda, Borg's housekeeper
Gunnar Björnstrand
Dr Evald Borg
Ingrid Thulin
Marianne Borg, Evald's wife
Bibi Andersson
Sara, a hitchhiker/ Sara, Isak's cousin
Björn Bjelvenstam
Viktor, a hitchhiking medical student
Folke Sundquist
Anders, a hitchhiking theology student
Gunnar Sjöberg
Sten Alman, an engineer
Gunnel Broström
Berit Alman, his wife
Max von Sydow
Henrik Åkerman, petrol-station owner
Ann-Mari Wiman
Eva Åkerman, Henrik's wife
Professor Helge Wulff
Public orator in Lund Cathedral
Gio Petré
Sigbritt, Isak's married sister
Per Skogsberg
Hagbart, the eldest Borg brother, aged around 20
Per Sjöstrand
Sigfrid, Isak's elder brother
Gunnel Lindblom
Charlotta, Isak's elder sister
Maud Hansson
Angelica, Isak's younger sister
Göran Lundquist
Benjamin, Isak's younger brother
Eva Norée
Anna, Isak's sister

Lena Bergman, Monica Ehrling
Kristina and Birgitta, Isak's twin sisters
Yngve Nordwall
Uncle Aron
Sif Ruud
Aunt Olga
Gertrud Fridh
Karin, Isak Borg's wife
Åke Fridell
Karin's lover
Else Fisher
Isak's mother as a young woman

Credits checked by Markku Salmi. The print of *Wild Strawberries* was specially acquired from Darvill Associates for the Film Classics series. Available on VHS in the UK on the Tartan Video label.

BIBLIOGRAPHY

Bergman, Ingmar, *Bilder* (Stockholm: Norstedts, 1990); published as *Images*, trans. Marianne Ruuth (London: Bloomsbury, 1994).

Bergman, Ingmar, *Laterna Magica* (Stockholm: Norstedts, 1987); published as *The Magic Lantern*, trans. Joan Tate (London: Hamish Hamilton, 1988).

Bergman, Ingmar, *Wild Strawberries: A Film*, trans. Lars Malmström and David Kushner (London: Lorrimer, 1986).

Binh, N. T., *Ingmar Bergman, Le magicien du Nord* (Paris: Gallimard, 1993).

Björkman, Stig (with Torsten Manns and Jonas Sima), *Bergman om Bergman* (Stockholm: Norstedts, 1970); published as *Bergman on Bergman, Interviews with Ingmar Bergman*, trans. Paul Britten Austin (London: Secker & Warburg, 1973).

Björkman, Stig and Olivier Assayas, *Conversations avec Bergman* (Paris: *Cahiers du Cinéma*, 1990); published as *Tre dagar med Bergman* (Stockholm: Filmkonst, 1992).

Cowie, Peter, *Ingmar Bergman, A Critical Biography* (London: Secker & Warburg, 1982).

Donner, Jörn, *Djävulens ansikte* (Stockholm: Aldus/Bonniers, 1962); published (in a revised version) as *The Films of Ingmar Bergman: From 'Torment' to 'All These Women'*, trans. Holger Lundbergh (New York: Dover, 1972).

Forslund, Bengt, *Victor Sjöström. Hans liv och verk* (Stockholm: Bonniers, 1980); published as *Victor Sjöström*, trans. Peter Cowie, with the assistance of Anna-Maija Marttinen and Christer Frunck (New York: Zoetrope, 1988).

Lagerlöf, Selma, *Körkarlen* (Stockholm: Bonniers, 1951).

Marker, Lise-Lone and Frederick, *Ingmar Bergman: Four Decades in the Theater* (Cambridge University Press, 1982).

Mosley, Philip, *Ingmar Bergman: The Cinema as Mistress* (London: Marion Boyars, 1981).

Törnqvist, Egil, *Filmdiktaren Ingmar Bergman* (Stockholm: Arena, 1993).

Wood, Robin, *Ingmar Bergman* (London: Studio Vista, 1969).

Zern, Leif, *Se Bergman* (Stockholm: Norstedts, 1993).